To John & [illegible]

With best wishes
from

Charles & Margaret.

It Took A Lifetime

Seamus Harkin

13/12/08

It Took A Lifetime
Seamus Harkin
Albertine Publications Copyright © 2008
Telephone +353 74 913 0833

Contents

Acknowledgements

I wish to say thanks to a number of people who were vital to the writing of this book. First of all I thank Tessie and all my family for all their help and encouragement and for putting up with me and all the proof reading at the beginning of my writings.

To Seamus Lafferty who was always there, often on the other side of the world, when I needed help putting my stories together. Thank you, Seamus, for all your contributions, particularly to the editing and layout. To my daughter-in-law Janet Harkin who guided me along at all times and whose advice and encouragement kept up my enthusiasm. Seamus and Janet worked together online in the laborious task of editing.

Thanks also to the many people who shared their stories with me and gave me the inspiration without which these writings would not have come together.

Thank you too to the many characters who feature in the stories and tales that makes up this book, real life people who enhanced the lives of everyone who knew them, and hopefully the people who will read of their lives in this book.

I dedicate this book to Tessie and all the family and to my grandchildren Jamie, Órlaith, Finn and Thómas who was just born a short time before the book went to print.

Introduction

The accounts and stories in this book are drawn from many aspects of my life and have been written over a period of ten years. I often used to tell stories of things that happened or things that I had seen while travelling around the countryside and would be urged to write them down. So now the stories are written between the covers of this book and I hope you find some of them interesting or amusing. Forgive me if I sometimes jump from one period of my life to another – I've found that's often the way with storytelling.

My son Paul asked me "Why are you writing this book?" and I thought that was a very good question.

All my life I have listened to stories told by my elders and neighbours, as well as many other people I've met along the way. But as well as listening, I also enjoy telling stories. What better way to pass on the way of life from the past than to write it down for future generations?

This book emerged from the desire within me to tell those tales of the past, in the hope that a few people at least will get a glimpse of how life was in the 20th century.

Foreword by Séamus Lafferty

THERE'S NOTHING QUITE LIKE EMIGRATING for making one appreciate the richness and depth of Irish tradition and culture. And, there's nothing quite like an annual visit home to put in focus how Ireland has and is changing. In a time of such rapid change, many of us seek out bastions that allow us to relive our past, and allow us to wallow in the memories of what seem, in hindsight at least, to have been simpler times. This book is one such bastion.

It's nearly 30 years ago now since I first saw Seamus Harkin perform on stage at a "social" in the hall on the Horn Head road in Dunfanaghy. Of all the varied jobs that Seamus has turned his hand to, none come easier to him than entertaining a dancing audience. That night he changed his baritone voice effortlessly from Neil McBride's Noreen Bawn to Johnny Cash's Folsom Prison Blues. Indeed, that night I couldn't have been more impressed had it been the Man in Black himself!

Harkin is a natural entertainer – both on the stage and off. In the pages that follow, you will come to realise that Seamus has played his entire life out on a stage – a stage across which many "characters" have passed. Before long, you'll realise that he's as much of a "character" himself as any he writes about.

Written in the style of a storyteller, and in the vernacular of his generation and his locality, this book is unpretentious in its prose, but rich in historical and entertainment value. Important milestones in the history of the Creeslough and Dunfanaghy areas of northwest Donegal punctuate a commentary on how life was lived, and how society has changed. The photographic memory of the author, combined with his raw and uncomplicated style of writing, serve to present us with a very vivid documentary of his life. Some of you will remember people, places and events; more of you will draw parallels with your own lives, and your minds will wander back; others will read these chapters for their unique and nuanced perspective on life in rural Ireland over the past 70 years.

I have very fond memories of Seamus and me travelling the 'highways and byways' of the county to play music together in pubs. I was mesmerised by the entertainer that Harkin was and is, and the apparent ease with which he presented himself on stage. When the "gig" was over, we'd load up the Liteace van, and night after night, the journey home was shortened by the stories and yarns for which Harkin is renowned. It is these stories, intermingled with his own life story, which are recorded in this volume.

Like many of his contemporaries, Seamus' formal education ended at age fourteen. As a result, Seamus is largely self-taught on anything he's ever done.

Unique among his siblings, Seamus never left home. In fact, he and Tessie, his wife of over 40 years, still reside on the farm on which he was born. As is fitting, Seamus and Tessie are immensely proud of their now-grown family; and relish the time they get to spend with their young grandchildren.

A big man in stature, a big man at heart, Seamus commands respect and authority. A man of strong religious faith and deep-rooted convictions, Seamus has long been involved in projects and organisations motivated to help and improve the community that has been his life-long home. He is a truly unique individual, with a unique life story, and a unique way of telling you about it.

It is an honour to recommend this book. It is an honour to know Seamus Harkin. I encourage you to read his life story and allow yourself to be consumed by the memories, by the wit, and by the charisma of an exceptional individual.

Séamus Lafferty, Ph.D.
Minneapolis, Minnesota, USA; and
Faugher, Dunfanaghy, Co. Donegal, Ireland.

Chapter 1 - The Early Years

It was a Tuesday but I don't know if the weather was good or bad that day. I do know that I was born on the 2nd of April 1935, in the townland of Derryart. The address was Derryart, Cashelmore, via Letterkenny, County Donegal. At that time Cashelmore was the local post office, one of the many rural post offices in the country, and Creeslough was our nearest village and the place where we did our shopping. When asked by someone where you were from, you always said Creeslough. Well, there was no point saying Derryart, as very few people would have heard of it.

The old house in Derryart is still there today and is a special place to me and all my family. It was also an important house for local people and other travellers who would often call in for a drink of water or tea, or maybe just to have a rest and a chat.

As a child I have great memories of the many people who came to our house. Some would stay for a short visit while others might stay for one night or longer. One such man who would come and stay sometimes for six months or more was Barney Diver.

I remember Barney coming to our house in the early autumn and staying right through the winter and spring. He would help with work on the farm for his keep.

When the nights grew longer people would visit each others' houses to chat and share stories, a practice known as 'raking'. One night in the week my mother and father would go a short way up the road to Ballymore to visit big Jim and Annie, my mother's parents, leaving us with Barney for company. As children, that was a night we looked forward to as we had good fun with Barney.

We liked the fact that although he was an adult we could relate to him too and the big treat we had on those evenings was Barney's biscuits. Barney had been in the army for a while and had learned some skills in the art of cooking. With this bit of knowledge and his own ingenuity he created his unusual biscuits, the main ingredient of which was porridge.

At that time porridge was a very important part of the diet in country areas and was eaten for breakfast and supper, and indeed at any other time of the day if a person was hungry and the porridge was handy. There was always a small pot of porridge sitting in the pantry and it could be eaten cold or warmed up if one preferred it that way. Our porridge was milled in Corcreggan Mill which is on the Falcarragh side of Dunfanaghy. Those days everyone grew their own oats or corn as it was called, and they got enough milled to keep them in oatmeal for porridge and bread. It was also mixed with potatoes to feed the hens and pigs.

The most common name for porridge was 'stir-a-bout', probably because it was boiled for about three hours and had to be continually stirred with a pot stick. That was often the job for granny sitting by the fire or anyone who might be fixing up the fire.

When I was a young boy a man who would have had 'a good drop to drink would often come into the house and say to my mother "Nan, have you any cold porridge in the house?" My mother would get the wee pot from the pantry and bring it out to him saying "Do you want me to heat some for you?" to which he would reply, "Nan, sure I have enough heat inside! Just give me the jug of milk." He would then proceed to pour the milk into the wee pot stirring it up and eating the lot. Sitting back in his chair he would fall asleep for maybe an hour. Upon waking, he would fill his pipe and head off home a much more sober man.

I started telling you about Barney's biscuits but got somewhat carried away about stir-a-bout and drunk men.

Anyway, Barney would get whatever porridge was left in the wee pot and mix it with milk until it was runny. He then got the old metal frying pan and hung it on the crook with some fatty bacon on it. The mixture was allowed to cook until there were some nice juices floating around in the pan. Large spoonfuls of the mixed porridge were then poured into the hot pan with the bacon fat. As he was doing this Barney would say "Mind your eyes for the sparks will be flying!"

After a few minutes on one side he turned the biscuits over and soon Barney's special biscuits were ready to eat. They were lovely and crunchy with a bacon flavour and we just loved them. That was our big treat for the week and we ate them until we were stuffed. At that time we thought no one could cook like Barney!

The little village of Creeslough was known all over Ireland and indeed further afield, because the singer and songwriter Percy French wrote a song about Creeslough entitled "The Emigrants Letter." The ending of each verse was "Where they're cutting the corn in Creeslough the day," so the song became better known as "Cutting the Corn in Creeslough." I remember visiting America one time and being asked where I was from and when I said Creeslough the person replied "That's the place where they cut the corn!" That was a typical response no matter where you were. Percy French put Creeslough on the map.

In later years Creeslough also became known on account of another person, Bridie Gallagher. Known as "The Girl from Donegal," Bridie, was from Ards, just over the road from me. She became very well known in the 1950's playing in venues from London to New York.

Other Creeslough people of note are Neil McBride and William Harkin. Neil was from Faymore and wrote many songs but is best known for "Noreen Bawn" and "The Hills of Donegal." William Harkin, a historian, author, songwriter and distant relation, was also from Creeslough village where his mother Sheila had a hotel. In 1891 William wrote a book entitled "Scenes and Antiquities of Donegal." He also composed songs, the best known of which is "Creeslough of The Lakes."

Creeslough was also known as the place that held the world record for growing potatoes – 35 tons and 6 cwt's per acre, grown in year of 1929.

In more recent times the little village of Creeslough was in the news when attention was focused on another Creeslough man, Bernard Lafferty. Bernard lived in Ards with his father Eddie and mother Angela, and he went to school there like any other young fellow of his time before spending a few years at the technical school in Letterkenny.

After school Bernard worked in the veneer factory at Derryart and, after his father died, he and his mother went to Glasgow. Sadly, his mother was killed in an accident and so he sold up the home place and went to America. Prior to leaving Bernard had always said he would make the big time.

When he first went to America he lived with his Aunt Maggie in Philadelphia and worked there for a short time. He did make it to Hollywood eventually and became friends with people like Peggy Lee, Elizabeth Taylor, Sharon Stone and many more.

Mixing in high-society he also met tobacco multi millionairess Miss Doris Dukes and became her butler and personal assistant. I think the rest of that story is well enough documented already. A number of films and television programmes were made about him and Miss Dukes. One such programme was shown on RTE entitled "Family Silver" in which I was interviewed about Bernard's life before he left Creeslough. Sadly, Bernard died young, in 1995, at the age of 50.

In the 1940's and 1950's there were many businesses in the village of Creeslough. As you entered the village from the Dunfanaghy side the first shop on your right was Mary Ann Harkin, also known as Mary Ann Friel; Mary Ann sold groceries and confectionery. Mickey Doherty resided with her and ran a hackney business. Next was Eddie Boyle who was an undertaker and had a hackney car as well. He also had a threshing mill and did ploughing through the parish for the farmers. Next was the forge, which was first owned by Bairds (known as the Dan Wannie's) and in later years it was run by the Doe Co-Op, the main smith being Neil Rodden from Terlin, assisted by Charlie Sweeney (Briney) from Rooskey. The next business was Ferry's Bar; next-door was Donal Tim.

Across the bridge the first business on the right was Willie Gallagher, a carpenter, and then there was a drapery shop owned by Wilkinson's. The Doe Cope (Co-Op) was next. It sold every thing from hardware to groceries including everything the farmer wanted and all the materials for building and outfitting a house. McFadden's Bar was next-door, later owned by Frank Sweeney, now McNulty's. Mandy Gallagher and his wife ran a tea house and their sons had a hackney service.

Across the street, the first business was Lafferty's Post Office and grocery shop. Below that was Billie Durning who sold a wide variety of items, from hardware to delf and all kinds of household goods. Next to that was Barney McGinley's. Barney's wife Mary ran a grocery shop while he worked in the forge out the back.

Charles John Durning was next, he ran the pub. Back across the bridge again on the right, was O'Donnell's hotel and next to that was Jammie Doherty. Jammie's shop was known as the pawnshop. I don't think he ever actually ran a pawnshop but he sold second hand clothes. Patsy Connaghan and Hudie Hunter had the next business, a grocery shop, and beside them was Joe Langan who was a butcher and cattle dealer.

At the end of the Magheroarty road Eddie McGinley from Faymore had a bottling store and later ran a butcher shop. The last business was Miss Cassidy's; she kept lace and small items of drapery. All in all there was a total of 20 businesses in the thriving village of Creeslough around the years 1950 to 1955. My home townland of Derryart was just two and a half miles from the village of Creeslough

Derryart and its surrounding townlands was a very pleasant and peaceful place in which to grow up even though we did not have many luxuries. There were five of us in the family, three boys and two girls, one other baby girl died at birth.

Mary is the oldest of the family, John was next and then myself. The little girl who died was a few years after me and then Nora was born and Hugh is the youngest. Our sister who died at birth was not talked about much, as was usual at that time. We only got to know about her much later in life.

I never cease to wonder how our parents managed to do it, but we didn't know that they had very little money, and sometimes none, when we were growing up. Home was always a happy place. We grew up in blissful ignorance of most of the hardships they must have encountered. The main message they got across to us was to waste nothing. That included time, money and materials.

My parents had a very strong faith and they passed that faith on with great conviction. Mass, the rosary and other forms of prayer were very important in their lives. It was very easy to grasp the message of "Love thy neighbour" as we all worked together and we were well used helping our neighbours.

My mother was the one who dished out the discipline. She had some very strict rules and, if not adhered to, the sally rod came down from the top of the dresser and you got it around the legs.

My father did not say much, but he always backed her up, and when he did speak, it was final. Obedience was very important, as was being truthful. Telling lies got you into the most trouble.

My mother's maiden name was Harkin. Given that both my father and mother were Harkin meant that we, their family, had the 'cure' for the mumps. It was always said by the old people that if your father and mother had the same surname, the family would be able to cure the mumps. To perform the cure, which I did a few times, you have to lead the person who has the mumps to the well and they have to drink three sups of water from the well in the name of Father, Son and Holy Spirit. If the person receiving the cure believes in it, then it will cure them.

Hugh was my father's name, but he was better known as Hughie. His father was John; he died six years before I was born. John's wife, Hannah, was a McGinley from Kilmacloo, up near the foot of Muckish. I remember my granny Hannah very well; she was a wonderful woman and was very good at composing little verses of poetry. My father had four brothers and three sisters; three brothers died in their teens around 1910. Uncle Johnny was the only one I remember on my father's side.

Johnny and my father, like many other young men of their time, were very much involved in the fight for freedom and Johnny spent much of that time around Glasgow getting guns to send back to the IRA. After 1922 Johnny joined the

Free State Army and was posted in several barracks throughout the country. He was stationed in Creeslough barracks (where Josephine Gallagher lives now) on the night Captain Cannon was shot. I often heard him tell the story of that fateful night.

It was the 10th of April 1923. It was a Fair night in Creeslough, and most of the people had gone home after completing their business of buying or selling at the fair so all was quiet in the little village. The civil war was almost over and no trouble was expected. There was a small number of soldiers in the barracks and Captain Cannon was in charge. Suddenly they were alerted by noise outside and people shouting, so they went to investigate. As Captain Cannon and my uncle Johnny approached the door, a shot rang out and, as Cannon was in front, he was shot and fatally wounded. While he lay on the floor Johnny said the Act of Contrition in his ear as he died. That was the last shooting of a Free State soldier in the civil war in Ireland – a shooting that was to have dire consequences. Four IRA men, who were in prison at the time for proposed offences against the State, were then shot in Drumboe.

Johnny retired from the army at the end of the 1940's and went to work for O'Brien's, the horse racing people in Kildare. After that he went to work with Irish Hospital Sweeps in Ballsbridge, Dublin, where he stayed until he retired back to Derryart about 1970. Johnny died in 1971.

My father's sisters were Maryann, Winifred and Katie. Winifred died in 1944 and Maryann lived in England for many years, before returning to Ireland around 1950. She lived with us in Derryart until her death in 1960. Katie married Dim Gillespie from Umerafad and died in 1995.

Jim and Annie Harkin were my maternal grandparents. They lived in the neighbouring townland of Ballymore, which is just across the river from Derryart. They had a large family, twelve of whom lived. One son, Dom, married Peggy McNulty from Crenera and set up home in Ballymore where they had fifteen of a family. You can imagine the impact that had on Ballymore, where there are still a large number of Harkins today.

The story was told about my father visiting Jim Harkin, which he did often. While visiting one time, he was given a little baby girl to nurse and Jim said to him, "Hughie, I will keep that girl for you," and so he did. That little girl was Nan, the girl he eventually married! But then, I do not know if you could believe that story because the two of them were great storytellers.

My grandfather was known as 'Big Jim'; he was a big man with big ways about him. He was the sort of man who commanded attention wherever he went and he always seemed to have an answer for everything. Growing up, my brother John and I thought he was the greatest man about the place. He always kept us entertained with all kinds of tales. I still remember many of the stories and recitations he taught us while working in the fields.

Big Jim was not an easy man to work for. You had to keep going and do the job well or you would hear about it. In those days there was no weed killer so weeds were pulled by hand. Weeding the potatoes, or the 'spuds' as we called them, and thinning and weeding the turnips were two of the main jobs (and most tedious) on the farm. Thinning the turnips was a slow, laborious task.

Big Jim had sixteen acres of land in Ards. This was once part of the Stewart's of Ards estate before it was divided among the farmers in the surrounding areas. It was about one-and-a-half miles from Ballymore to this field and we would walk there carrying our bottles of milk and bag of home-made bread.

The drills were 'grubbed' the day before which made them narrower and, with any luck, some of the weeds would have been up-rooted already. The drills were about one hundred and fifty yards long and they stretched up the hill and over the brow. Somehow, it always seemed worse if you could not see the other end of the drill.

In preparation for the work, we wound bags around our legs to protect our knees from the stones as we went along. We had to creep along between the two drills, in what was known as 'the shuch', weeding and thinning the turnips as we went.

Big Jim was a very shrewd man and he knew how to handle two young fellows. To relieve the monotony of the job, he would tell us stories, poems and recitations while we crept up the drills. Six drills up and six down, then it was time for the milk with bread and jam. He would always promise us something big if we finished in good time but he mostly got out of it somehow and we never caught on to him.

As I grew older I always felt that this work was good training for perseverance. It trained the mind to accept and handle monotonous tasks and to cope with repetitive work.

Here is one of the recitations Big Jim taught us while working in the fields. It tells the story of a man who, after returning from the Boer War, talked of the strange place names and officers he came across. His wife became obsessed with these names and when their first baby boy was born she wanted to call him after these names.

THE BOER WAR

The war the war the blooming war has ruined my wife and wane,
From Macruga to Majuba she has the Transvaal on the brain.
And when to christen our first child last Sunday week we tried,
When the Parson called, "What's this child's name?" then my old girl replied
Chorus:
>	The baby's name is Kitchener, Kruger, Methuen, Meevach, White,
>	Cronje Plummer, Powell, Majuba, Gattacrea, Warren, Collenca Caroga
>	Mafeking, Kimberly, Blobs, the Union Jack, and Fighting Mack,
>	And Lady Pretoria Bobs.

The Parson said, "Such names I can't upon this infant pop,"
But my wife broke his Roland Belt and smashed his Spion Cop.
She jumped upon his Croon stead and she never made a miss,
Says she, "I'll burst your armour train if you don't think of this."
>	Repeat Chorus

She tore the Parson's flag of truce; she burst his Jacob's stall,
She run her Moder River up through his shrapnel.
She kicked his mounted infantry till his Bloemfontein was sore,
Then she did a flanking movement, and she shouts it out once more.
>	Repeat Chorus

Paul Kruger was the President of South Africa at that time and Piet Cronje was a
General. Bloemfontein was the capital of the Orange Free State.

Big Jim was a natural storyteller and when he told a story, he did so with great
gusto. Dinny and Big Jim lived next door and they were known as "The Franks"
as their father was Big Frank. Though a quiet man, Dinny had great character.
When talking to Dinny you could be forgiven for thinking that he knew nothing
and believed everything he heard, but you would be very much mistaken.

Big Jim would tell him very far-fetched stories and it seemed, when the story
was being told, that Dinny believed the whole thing. He would nod his head in
agreement and talk in great wonderment about the story. Then Big Jim would
leave, very pleased with himself thinking that Dinny had swallowed the whole
story.

I was with Dinny one day helping him to spread farmyard manure, or 'dung' as
we called it. Now there was a job-and-a-half! The manure, mostly from cows,
was taken to the field with the horse and cart and left off in small heaps in the
drills for the potatoes. It then had to be spread evenly along the drills before the
potatoes were set. Anyhow, Big Jim came into the field and began to tell Dinny
one of his tall stories. When the story was finished and Big Jim walked off down

the field, Dinny leaned on the 'grape', dropped a big spit on the ground and looked after him saying, "He's a droll man but there's no harm in him."

I could fill a book with stories about Dinny Frank. He was the complete opposite to Big Jim. Dinny's answer to most questions about work being done around the farm was "It'll do rightly." I loved to work with Dinny because he never scolded you for not doing the work properly. It was while working with him that I opened my first drills with the horse and plough.

Opening drills for potatoes was a very precise job. The old men were very particular about the overall look of the drills. They had to be the right size, the right depth and above all, as straight as a gunshot. But Dinny wasn't worried about making the drill straight; he would always say "Sure, they will grow as well in crooked drills as straight ones."

Big Jim once told a story about a young fellow who worked in a neighbour's house. In those days, he was known as a "servant boy." Farmers would hire a servant boy to help with the work on the farm, especially when they did not have a family of their own. This young fellow was working in a certain farmhouse and was not too well informed on women's things. The woman of the house was having a baby and the nurse had just arrived.

Now the nurse was a big tall woman dressed in black who travelled the countryside on a bicycle with her black bag on the carrier. The bicycle was fitted with threads going from the mudguard down to the axel of the back wheel. This was to keep her long coat from becoming entangled in the spokes of the wheel. Such a device was common on ladies bicycles at the time. No-one seemed to know this woman's name, everyone knew her as "the nurse."

Well, as I said, she arrived at this house and was talking to the woman who was expecting the baby and making arrangements for the birth. Johnny the servant boy came in to the house and wanted to see the woman. The nurse explained to him that he could not see her because she was in bed having a baby. Johnny said "Well sure I'll come in and give you a hand." In order to keep Johnny from coming into the room she had to think of something she could get him to do to keep him occupied. So, she got a bucket and told him to go to the well and take back a bucket of water. Johnny was back in a flash with the water so she took it into the room and threw it out the back window. She then gave him two buckets to slow him down.

All through the labour Johnny kept carrying the water. After about two hours the nurse said he could stop carrying the water now as the baby was born. Johnny went to see the woman and the baby and was pleased with a job well done. The next evening Johnny was standing at the crossroads with a few of the men when the nurse passed on her bicycle. Someone said "I wonder where she's going this evening" and Johnny said "I don't know where she's going, but God help the man who has to carry the water!"

It was a common occurrence in our house through the 1940's and early 1950's to have travellers calling in the evenings to get a night's lodgings – we called them tramps. That name isn't politically correct now but at the time they were quite pleased and proud of it as they told of the long 'tramps' they had around the countryside.

These men would call on a winter's evening just at dark and in time for their evening tea. They would ask very politely if they could get lodgings for the night. I never knew my father and mother to turn anyone away except one or two who were very unmannerly.

Two men who called very regularly were called McGoldrick and Charlie Devine. McGoldrick was a big man who carried a blackthorn stick with an inch of lead on the end of it. He would get his tea after arriving and then later he would get supper with the family. He never slept in the house but would go out to the barn and make a bed out of straw and use big jute bags for blankets. John and I would light the hurricane lamp and accompany him to the barn and wait until he was in bed. We would then take straw to the byre to fodder the cows and we often stopped at the barn on our way back to hear him say the Rosary aloud.

Charlie Devine had no legs and went around in a box with pram wheels on it. He pushed himself along with the tops of two spade handles with nails in them. He would sleep on a "shake down" in the kitchen, which was an old mattress, kept for such an occasion and laid down close to the fire. When the family went to bed and the fire was raked he would be as snug as a bug in a rug. In the morning these men would get their breakfast with the family and then they were on their way maybe to return a few months later.

There was a few other men who would come occasionally. One was called Willie Caol (also known as Thin Willie), another was Frank Long and then there was "The Tory Man." A man used to come who wore top hat and tails and he played a clarinet. He would never come into the house but sat on the flag outside the door and played his clarinet. He had to get paid a halfpenny for every tune; I never knew his name.

The following recitation was written long before my time. I am sure it was Neil McBride's way of listing all the names of the people who travelled around at that time. Most of the characters in Neil's list were known as beggars.

THE BEGGARS OF DOE

Come pick the wax out of your ears, and keep your whiskers straight,
It's about a jolly begging crew this tale I will relate,
About the Christmas time of year the beggars did unite,
So they all agreed to come with me and spend a jolly night.
The dreary winters day had closed the night was gathering fast,
A cool December wind arose and blew a bitter blast,
The snow came down in blinding flakes on cottage sty and byre,
When I sat me down with right goodwill beside my kitchen fire.
I took my dudeen off the hob to take a hearty smoke,
And longed for someone to come in, that we might crack a joke.
My wee dog Sailor barked aloud, outside my cabin door,
And soon a human form appeared and stood upon the floor.
It was Paddy Na Gauge his hair was grey his step slow and firm,
And who came grunting after that but trotting John the Worm.
Then Jimmy Quinn came running in, he'd neither sit nor stand,
And after him came Neety the red whiskered praying man.
Then Silly Willy Higgins came along with Biddy Bucky,
The beggar from Glenswilly came along with Mary Tricky.
Then Paddy the Rope and Willie the Lick to come they did not fail,
And then came Charlie the Marbles with Mary Burndale.
The ballad singer Gorm came, with tinkers half-a-dozen,
Fat legs the beggar man his wife and seven cousins.
The pots and pans did rattle then without the least delay,
And the Women then got cracking
with the making the tae.
The pipes were filled and handed 'round among the ragged crowd,
Then the ballad singer Gorm began to sing aloud.
When the song he sung was finished, he got loud applause and din,
Then Paddy Poy the piper and his wife came paddling in.
A dance, a dance and chorus round the ragged circle ran,
He played a tune and very soon the dancing it began.
Paddy the Geake forgot his age and danced an Irish Jig,
While lazy Brinnie Mickey danced the Killygordan Rig.
The next for dancing on the floor was the ballad singer Gorm,
And as he danced the Highland fling, he tramped on John the Worm.
Then trotting John did curse and damn and challenged him to fight,
Saying you ballad singer blackguard you're drunk again tonight.
Then the tinkers all assembled round the ballad singer Gorm,

But the beggars all declared they would fight for John the Worm.
The piper bolted for the door for he being no way slack,
But Paddy the Rope pursued him first and quickly brought him back.
Saying, "You got your tae and you must stay!" and he tied him to a post.
While the piper pale and trembling stood, you'd think he was a ghost.
The praying man said, "Lord above look down upon these fools.",
"Amen," said Charlie the Marbles, and blinded him with a stool.
The praying man then let an oath and quickly dropped his prayer
And soon the floor was covered o'er with bits of skin and hair.
The tinkers fought like warriors bold, to battle marching on
When who the devil darted in but clever Willie John.
He said "I am a bold JP. Indeed it is a fact!"
Then mounted high upon a stool he read the riot act
The praying man then raised his hand and humbly prayed for peace,
When Gorm bold withdrew his men and the fighting it did cease.
When the battle it was over they missed old Willie Higgins,
Says Gorm "I cannot see him anywhere around the diggings."
Then every man the search began, when in comes Brinnie Mickey,
Saying "He's out there in the barn colluding with Mary Tricky."
They all shook hands in friendship then and to the drink did fall
You couldn't find a jollier crowd from Cork to Donegal.
So now the night was finished, it was at the break of day,
With broken bones and blackened eyes the job lot marched away.

AUTHOR: NEIL MCBRIDE

My father went to Scotland to work in about 1942. World War Two was still on
and work in Ireland was very scarce and there was not much money around. He
went to work with a farmer called Mackey at Gretna Green. Vincent McFadden
from Swillybrin and Mickey Sweeney from Kildarragh were on the same farm.
My father used to wire money home every two weeks. The postman would tell us
that a wire was in Annie Hunter's post office and then my mother would go and
collect the money.

I remember the first time he went away we, as children, did not understand why
he had to go. My mother put on a good face for our benefit but you could see
she missed him terribly, as did we all. He went away in the late spring or early
summer and did not return until Christmas. I can still remember that Christmas
Eve waiting on the bus to stop. There were always a lot of buses on Christmas
Eve and we had almost given up hope when the sixth bus passed. You can
imagine our excitement when the next bus stopped and there was Daddy walking
down the bus.

As children I suppose we never really understood how much my mother missed him while he was away. We missed him as a father but she missed him as husband and partner. So, for the first hour or so after he'd arrived there was a lot of catching up to do on all the news and the things that had happened while he'd been away. There was big excitement for us, and especially when he produced the presents that he had brought us back for Christmas.

I remember the Christmas of 1942 when he had a clock with him. It had the picture of the blacksmith at Gretna Green on the face of it. The little blacksmith was in the shape of a leprechaun and each time the clock ticked he hit the anvil with his little hammer. He also had a book entitled "The Gretna Blacksmith Story." It is signed R.B. Mackinnon, the last priest of Gretna, and dated the 30th June 1940.

That clock and book are still in the house and they remind me of those Christmases of long ago. My father would stay at home then until February or March when the ploughing was done and some of the crop had been put in, at which point he would leave again for another nine months.

He left Gretna in about 1947 and went to work in Pitlochry in Perthshire where there was a dam for a hydroelectric scheme being built. A lot of Donegal people worked there, many of them from Creeslough. While my father was there the dam was flooded and nearly everything was washed away. He was not a young man at that time and the work was very heavy but he stayed there for three years. The main foreman on the job was McBride from Faymore, Creeslough. He returned home about 1949 and thankfully did not have to leave home to work any more as things began to pick up in Ireland after that. He composed a recitation about the flooding.

THE PITLOCHRY DAM

The Pitlochry Dam is in debt now they say,
That's what I was told when I went there the other day
And for to redeem it they took a poor way
When they paid off the messenger boy wee Johnny Grey.
The word came through from Great London town
To pay off all the McBrides on the job to be found,
The Boyles and the Doogan's and the Harkin's also
So up to the office we all had to go.
And when we went up, there was nobody in
So we sent Punch Doogan to have a look 'round,
He came back as he went; he says, "They are all crooks
We'll just walk inside and demand our books."

McBride then, says he, "Can I have a meeting this evening at three
And have the whole facts for them there for to see?"
They held the meeting that evening at three on the clock
There was one man, a great man, they nearly forgot.
That man was Mahoney, he was over in the trench
They had to pull him out with Paddy Herrighty's wrench
And when he got out, he was a scare man
Says he, "I wish to God I'd never been seen in this dam.
For it is my opinion, someone's acting the rogue
I think we had better send for old Charlie Logue."
When Charlie arrived there wasn't one to be seen
Only wee Daniel Shussie and big Hughie Green.
Says Charlie, "They think that I'm a quare bum
 I'll dodge over to Fisher's and have a few nips of rum."
But the trouble was settled and we were working again
When a thundercloud burst and down came the rain.
The dam it was flooded, and left them all in suspense
Says McLaughlin to McBride, "This will add more to the expense."
Aye, the dam it was flooded, not a pile to be seen
When Collins and Pat Cannon arrived on the scene.
Says Collins, "I think I'll go back for my coat,
And I'll send Paddy Herrighty down with the boat."
Paddy arrived in a very short time
He says to Pat Cannon, "We'll need a long line.
We'll save tools, planks and batons and other things as well
We might get the rest tomorrow, down at Dunkeld."
These three Jolly sea men they bordered the board
And up through the dam with great speed they did float.
They piled on planks and batons till they couldn't take any more
Captain Herrighty gave orders to pull to the shore.
Success to Paddy Herrighty and likewise his crew
Between planks and batons they saved quite a few.
Then Johnny came up in a hell of a steer
Saying, "Did any of you see wee Daniel about here,
I have a big bay to scabble and it's now getting late
And I wanted it to tomorrow for the concrete."
Daniel spoke up, "That's man of great skill,"
Says he, "I was scabble with any man at the foot of this hill,
But since this trouble arose, I have got a bit slack
And if times don't change I think I will jack.
I will go over to Ireland and there I will bide
For I'm sure of a job with wee Charlie McBride."

Bad luck to big Harry I wonder where he is now
It was him and Cordon Leyden that raised the whole row.
But if ever he comes back here, he won't be as clever
For I'll get Johnny to throw him in the river
Now I'll end my story with a word of success,
I hope every man in the dam will do his best
And when I return from my own native land
I hope everything will be hopping on the Pitlochry Dam.

AUTHOR HUGHIE HARKIN

Chapter 2 - 1947

1947 was a year I remember well and for one reason, snow. It has been talked about since as the year of the big snow. The snow that year started near the end of February and continued until the beginning of April.

Like every young fellow I loved to see the snow coming. There was something magical about getting up in the morning to see everything covered in snow. It also meant, of course, that the school would be closed for a few days and anything that caused the school to close for any length of time had to be good. Normally the snow would last for one or two weeks at the most and we usually had a few snowfalls during the winter. But the snow of 1947 was different to anything we had seen. It seemed as if it was never going to end and I think it cured me of longing for snow for some time.

For the first two weeks it was great fun. Every day we were out with our sleighs and, as there was not much traffic on the roads those days, we were able to sleigh on the Derryart Bray without any danger. Whatever few cars and lorries were on the road had a terrible problem getting up the hills. We thought it was amusing to see the lorries getting stuck in the snow, but I'm sure it was not amusing for the unfortunate drivers.

After a new fall of snow it was almost impossible for lorries to go up the Derryart Bray. Often the drivers had to stay in our house overnight and, with some grit and gravel thrown on the road, next day they were able to proceed. But, as the weeks passed with no sign of a thaw, people started to tire of it, even the children.

Everywhere was now frozen over, the lakes and rivers and even the sea was starting to freeze. The birds were dying for want of food; the sea gulls and crows were the worst hit.

We had a thrashing mill in the barn and people came to get their corn thrashed. The corn had to be transported by horse and cart and that was not easy as the roads were very slippery. When it was thrashed, the resulting grain had to be cleaned and bagged; this was achieved by putting the corn through fans. The fans were turned by hand, which blew the chaff from the grain, and it riddled it and took out the light grain and weed seeds. This waste grain was thrown across the wall at the edge of the forest and was a welcome feast for the birds.

The farmers saved many birds but, as the weeks passed, the big birds like the seagulls, crows, blackbirds and thrushes were getting very weak. I remember seeing the seagulls and crows landing in the farmyard to eat the grain left behind from the threshing and not being able to take off again. They usually sat there until they died.

Another bird that was severely hit by the frost was the heron. All the lakes were frozen and many people went to Sessiagh Lough, near Portnablagh, on a Sunday to slide and play on the ice. Eric Stewart and Kern Sweeney even took their motor vehicles out on the lake and drove around the island. However, we were not allowed to go on the lake as it was considered very dangerous. It was said at the time that the ice was over one foot thick.

By the end of March the snow was still there with no sign of it going away. Every other year most of the ploughing would have been done by this time. Back then, the horses did all the farm work and the ploughing was the biggest job on the farm. A lot of preparation was necessary to get the plough and the harness for the horses ready.

The wintery sun shone down every day at the back of the house and, with the shelter of the dwelling house and out houses, it was a pleasant place to do some work on the old plough. The plough was taken out of the cart shed to the middle of the yard and all the nuts and bolts checked and oiled. It was important to oil the nuts so they could be loosened. Two of the main items on the plough were the 'sock' and the 'cooter' (its proper name was the coulter); they had to be taken to the forge to be pointed.

I always loved going to the forge, which was just across the road from Doe Chapel. It was owned by Robert John Stewart, and in later years the business was carried on by Samuel Stewart. Anytime I was missing from the house, I was either in Doherty's or up in Robert John's forge.

So off I went with the sock and the coulter in a bag to get them pointed. As I was approaching the forge, I could hear the ring of the anvil in the still, frosty air. The door was closed and I could hear voices inside so I knew there was a good number of people in the forge. Opening the door and walking in from the bright snow, I was almost blinded and it took a few minutes for my eyes to adjust to the relative darkness inside the forge. The men standing around spoke and Robert said "Well gasur, do you like the snow?"

There was one horse in the forge and Robert was making the shoes. About eight men stood around the forge waiting to get some job or other done. As there was not much work to be done due to the snow, it was a good place to spend the day. Everything was talked about, from world affairs to local gossip. There was always some 'character' there who would keep the crack going and Robert John would act as a kind of chairman. He knew how to 'steer' the conversation to get the best results. There would always be someone in the group who would believe the stories and go home and tell them. This, of course, was the object of the whole conversation.

The men carried on talking amongst themselves, occasionally referring to me as "Hughie Harkin's young fella" and Robert would say "Now Hughie could tell a good story."

The fire was glowing red as the bellows pumped the air into it. The bellows were mounted behind the fire; they were about eight feet long and made of leather. A long shaft of timber was connected to a cross bar above the bellows with a chain connected to the lower frame of the bellows. This shaft had a cow's horn on the end of it as a handle and the blowing was done by pulling down on the shaft. I loved to pull the bellows and when I was in the forge on my own, Robert would ask me to do the job. As there were a big crowd this day, I was too shy to push myself in. I kept moving towards the bellows and after a while Robert said, "Let that gasur pull them bellows for I know he's wild to get at them."

Robert had the iron in the fire for making the horse shoes and every time I pulled the bellows the heart of the fire became bright red with a blue tinge to the flames. After a few minutes he took out the iron, which was almost white at this stage, and hammered it into shape over the end of the anvil. As he hammered it, the bright sparks flew all around the forge, falling to the floor as they died. Slowly the shoes took shape and when they were finished he punched the seven holes in each one for the nails.

The next job was the cleaning of the horse's hooves. To do this the old shoes were removed and the hooves trimmed. The sole of the foot, which was called the frog, was cleaned and any foreign matter like small stones were removed. Now it was time to fit the shoes. The shoes were taken from the fire bright red and Robert had a special tool that he drove into one of the holes in the shoe. Then, lifting the shoe, he placed it on the horses hoof making sure it was in the right position, and burned the shape of the shoe into the hoof. As the hot shoe burned its shape into the hoof, the smoke filled the forge bringing with it the strong smell of the horse's burning hoof.

The fitting of the shoe was a very skilful job. A good blacksmith could correct a horse's foot if needed. If a horse walked inwards on his front foot, the smith would burn it down on the outside and level it. The same thing could be done with the hind legs if they needed correction. As I said, this was a job that was very skilful and needed a lot of experience. It was known as 'singeing'. This looked cruel, but the horse felt nothing as the hoof has no feeling. When the shoe was seated, it was then nailed on. The final job was to clinch the nails and file down the outside of the hoof and the horse was ready for the road.

The next job was for a man who had a bag of harrow pins which had to be pointed and some of them lengthened. After a few more jobs it was my turn. It did not take Robert long pointing the sock, but the coulter was very badly worn and Robert said "Gasur, I'll have to put a piece on to it." With my job completed there was no reason to stay any longer so I headed for home.

Another memory I have of 1947 is the marriage of my Aunt Rose from Ballymore to Andy Boyle from Magherablade, Creeslough. It was the first big wedding for me, well we thought it was big at that time but it wasn't really by today's standards. It all seemed very glamorous and exciting. The wedding breakfast was held in the old home in Ballymore then all the adults went off for a drive around the countryside, as was the custom at the time, while the young ones waited patiently until they returned.

I remember as they were returning the snow was starting to fall – the beginning of the big snow of 1947. Another big meal was prepared and enjoyed; then the dancing started. The music and dancing was held in the house next-door which was Dinny Harkin's (Frank's) and the music was played by Hughie McLaughlin, better known as Hughie Anton. The big hit at the time was "Give Me Five Minutes More", which Hughie seemed to play all night. The dancing did not finish until six o'clock in the morning and it was a very memorable occasion for all us young ones.

Chapter 3 – School

I left Faugher National School when I was fourteen years of age and that was my book learning finished. From then on, anything I learned was at the 'University of Life'.

My school days were very tough; when I went to school my first teacher was Miss McGowan. To us children she looked like an old woman, but I found out later she was only a young girl at the time, about twenty-two.

On a cold frosty winter morning, after walking a mile and a half your hands were frozen. The greeting you got, just because you were a few minutes late, was to stand there with your hands out-stretched to receive 'six of the best' with a big stick. And then you were supposed to sit down at your desk and try to write an essay or do sums! I suppose in those days teachers themselves were taught to pass on knowledge primarily through fear. But enough said about that; I could write a whole book about what went on at school and the cruelty there.

When I was growing up my parents and other adults told me that my school days would be the best days of my life. I must say those years themselves were good and I have very happy memories of those long gone days. Life at home and working on the farm were happy, carefree days and the summers back then seemed to be never-ending. But the time spent in school, now that was a different story. I would have to say I never enjoyed any of it.

The only good thing about my school days was the friends I made, loyal friendships that have lasted throughout my life. The one thing I am glad about is that I don't hold any grudges against anyone for the hardships I endured at school. After all, the worst thing we got was a 'clout' of a stick, which was just the way things were at that time but thankfully, not any more.

Some people go through their lives blaming things that happened to them when they were young for the problems they have today. Teachers and parents dished out discipline as they thought best. Teachers knew no other way of getting their point across, except through fear. And, after all, I don't think it did me any harm. Sure, maybe if I'd had a lot of book learning I may have ended up in a big job that wouldn't have suited me. But instead, the life I have had has been mostly of my own choosing and I'm happy to say I have enjoyed every day of it.

Walking home from school was good fun; it was one and a half miles but we didn't think it very long. On the way home, we got into all sorts of mischief.

Some times it was fighting, but mostly it was just playing games and exploring things along the way. Bullying was never a problem. If there was a grievance between two boys there was a fight set up and they settled their differences, after which they were pals again.

In the springtime we would play marbles along the road on a smooth sandy strip. Each player would place one marble on a square drawn on the sand, called 'the bed'. The marbles were made of clay and were different colours. The big one was called a 'crock' and the line drawn in the sand about six or eight feet from the bed, was called the 'butt'. The object of the game was to throw the crock at the bed and try to knock one of the marbles off the bed. Each person got a throw and you got to keep the marbles you knocked off. Everyones ambition was to have the biggest bag of marbles at the end of the season.

I remember the 'Far East' magazine that used to come into the school and each family took a copy home. The magazine raised money for 'The Black Babies' and one of the ways of raising money was known as the 'Penny Dabs'.

Penny dabs were sheets of paper divided into little squares and each time you stuck a pin in the square, you paid one penny. On our way home from school we used to call at houses selling the penny dabs. We all used to line up at the Rectory door in Ballymore and ring the bell; Mrs Staunton came out with her fist full of pennies and each caller got two pennies and their two squares 'dabbed' before it was on to the next house. Not all of them were as generous as Mrs Staunton.

Another big attraction on our way home from school were the apple gardens. By the time we returned to school after the summer holidays, most of the apples were all picked but there was one garden where some apples would still be on the trees, it was owned by Johnny Mac Intyre. Johnny lived alone and used to be working in the fields which gave us a chance to get some apples. But some of the children who didn't go into the garden would often tell Johnny that his garden was being raided.

I remember one day when he landed on horseback and caught us in the garden, red handed. We started running, with him after us on the horse; it was like something out of a cowboy film. Of course, the chase was all part of the fun.

After such adventures the dinner was always a welcome sight when we arrived home. After eating as much as we could, it was out to the fields to work at something or do chores around the farmyard. We were never bored. Spring and autumn were the busiest times of year on the farm. When the work was all finished outside, we came into the house for the evening tea and then it was down to the homework. I was never very good at the books and made every excuse not to do my homework – inevitably I would pay the price at school the next day!

The old kitchen was a pleasant place when the single burner oil lamp was lit on a winter's evening and the curtains drawn, closing out the dark winter night. When it was first lit the flame had to be kept low until the globe heated, as it would crack if turned up too soon. Soon enough it was slowly turned up and a golden glow filled the room, making it seem warm and cosy as the whitewashed walls reflected the light all around the kitchen. The turf fire added to the scene as it threw a flaring light across the flag floor.

One school day stands out from the rest – that was the day that a war plane had to make an emergency landing on Killyhoey Strand, near Dunfanaghy. I don't remember when it was and there seems to be some confusion now regarding the date and year. Some records say it was on the 16th June 1942 while another says it was the 2nd May 1943.

I recall returning into the school at Faugher on that day after playtime and hearing the roar of a plane coming from the Creeslough direction. It flew over Faugher hill, heading towards Portnablagh. We could hear it roaring even louder as it disappeared out of sight, then all went eerily quiet. Master Sean Gallagher from Gweedore, who was the principal teacher at the time, took the older children up to the top of Faugher hill to see where the plane went. Some time later the party returned and told those eagerly waiting back at the school that the plane had landed on Killyhoey strand.

While doing some research on that day I talked with Andrew McGinley from Ramonnaghan, Dunfanaghy and he confirmed that it was on Tuesday the 16th June, 1942. Not alone did he know the day and date, but he knew what he was doing on that day. He said "I was left in charge of boiling the big pot of potatoes for the dinner and when I took the pot outside to team the water off them I heard the roar of the plane coming in over the hill. It then flew over Killyhoey strand and after a few circles it flew towards Carrigart disappearing over Breaghy. The next thing I heard was the sound if it coming back over Faugher hill when it proceeded to fly low over the beach and came to rest in the middle of Killyhoey strand".

By Sunday the news had spread throughout the parish and it seemed everyone was heading for Killyhoey to see the plane. As most people had never seen a plane up close before, this was a big event. My father took us to see it and I remember being very excited to see this big flying machine just sitting there on the beach. We weren't allowed too close as the Local Defence Force were guarding it and keeping people back. There was a lorry load of jerry cans of petrol and volunteers were carrying the cans to the plane for refuelling but, of course, we were too small to help with the cans.

The next day the plane was towed to the end of the beach to give it as long a run as possible and, sure enough, it took off successfully, heading out over Horn Head and away. One boy I know who stayed off school that morning to see the plane take off was Tommy Stewart from Sessiagh. I don't think he was ever caught 'mitching' that day but I don't think he'll mind me telling tales on him now.

On leaving national school at the age of 12 or 13 most country children went to work on the family farm and very few went on to secondary school. It was only those who could afford it who were able to send their children to higher education.

In our family three went on to secondary school. Mary went to the Technical school in Letterkenny while Nora went to the Loreto Convent and then went on to a commerce school in Cavan. Hugh attended St. Eunan's college and then entered Maynooth seminary to study for the priesthood. He stayed there until one year before being ordained, at which time he decided the priesthood was not for him. I always say that John and I must have been very clever as we did not need any more formal education.

Mary went to America in 1952; she married a Letterkenny man named Joe Mc Glynn, and raised five of a family. John was in the Insurance business where he worked all his life. He married Dymphna McFadden from Milford and had four of a family. In 1968 he moved to Wicklow where he remained until his death in 2005. Nora went to work in Dublin where she met and married a Dublin man named Jerry Butler; they have four of a family and they still live in Lucan. Hugh worked for a few years with the I.F.A. in Leitrim. He then went to work with Avonmore creameries in Kilkenny and it was there he met and married Mary Dunne. They had two girls. They then moved to Dublin where Mary sadly died in 2003. Hugh and the girls still live there.

Throughout the 1970's rural national schools were being closed and the children taken by bus to the nearest village to a larger school. At the time the Government thought this was the right course of action, and no doubt it was intended to save money. Any parent who objected was told they were behind the times. So, many little country schools were closed and sold, and another part of rural life ended.

Faugher was the local school for the children from Derryart to Portnablagh; it was a two-teacher school with near enough 40 pupils. Sure enough the time came when we were notified that the school was to be closed and the children sent by bus to Dunfanaghy, where we were told there would be better facilities.

This decision was not well received by the parents but we thought that, with so many other schools in the same boat, we didn't have much of a chance of keeping ours open.

One Sunday two of the parents, Jimmy Lafferty and Tony Friel from Faugher, came to me and said, "What are we going to do about the school?" As parents ourselves we were naturally concerned about what was best for our children and we realised that we had to do something to save our school. So we visited the rest of the parents who were also in favour of keeping Faugher School open.

Many meetings followed, and our determination to keep our school from going the same way as so many others grew. The Department of Education made strong efforts to try and persuade us to go along with the plan to amalgamate with Dunfanaghy School and continually asked us to give up the idea of keeping our own school. They even threatened that we would loose our government funding if we continued with our campaign.

But we were not going to be deterred so we carried on with the fight; we told them that we would raise our own funding if it came to it. We were fortunate that the teachers in the school supported us. The teachers at the time were Mrs Caitlin O'Reilly who lived in Dunfanaghy and Mrs Mary Clark from Carrigart. After nearly a year of negotiations we won our battle and our little school in Faugher was saved from closure. I'm proud to say it's still going strong today.

In the years that followed we raised money to renovate the school and bring it up to date, with central heating, new desks and floor covering. The teachers at that time were Master Michael Murray and Mrs Rosaleen Kacperski and they organised and ran very successful concerts with the children, which raised a lot of money as well as being very beneficial to the children, building character and confidence.

In 1986 we installed a computer in the school. It was a BBC compact computer and was the top of the range at the time; I still have one and it is still working. I think we may have been the first national school in the county, if not the country, to have a computer. The school has added on more classrooms since and has been an outstanding success and Michael is still there and Rosaleen has just retired.

Never one to be outdone, I got my own BBC Compact computer in 1985. It was very advanced for its time. I remember when I first got it; I sat down with the manual and began to study. The first few pages seemed a waste of time, so I glossed over them and soon moved on to the serious stuff, which described how to do some programs. I followed the instructions to the letter but, no matter what I did, nothing happened so I gave up the first night, extremely frustrated.

But the next night I happened to notice a note on the inside front page which read, 'Please read the first pages carefully before attempting to operate the computer'. In the middle of about the third page, the instruction in bold print was, 'No programme will be activated without first pressing Return.' It makes me think that knowing just ninety five percent of a subject can be very dangerous, as the most important fact might be in the unknown five percent.

Chapter 4 - Aunt Katie

Every summer I looked forward to going to Aunt Katie's for a week during the school holidays. Aunt Katie lived in Umerafad, on the other side of Creeslough, and her husband was Dim Gillespie. Dim was a lovely man and was great at telling jokes. He was always in good humour; at least he was with me. Dim and Katie lived in a little three-purling cottage, half the roof was thatched and the other half was covered with felt. They kept the little house white-washed outside and inside.

After a number of years of marriage, they had one son called Paddy, but in the early years I had the house to myself and got all the attention. Mind you, Aunt Katie would not let me away with very much, but I could always get around her. The little kitchen had a hearth fire and a stone flag floor. There was one room on either side of the kitchen, a "one up and one down" as they would say. The kitchen table sat in front of the little four-pained window and the cupboards sat around the walls with the bag of white flower sitting near to the fire.

A number of holy pictures hung around the walls and in pride of place was the picture of the Sacred Heart. This picture hung on the back wall to the left of the fire. It was a big picture of Jesus with a very impressive face and no matter where you were in the kitchen you thought his eyes were looking at you. Underneath the picture hung a lovely brass lamp, which had a red globe and was kept burning night and day. If oil was scarce, this lamp would take priority over any other lamp and every Saturday it was polished with Brasso.

Along the back wall, beneath the picture, was the "settle bed" – a very useful piece of furniture. By day it was used as a seat and at night it could be opened out as a bed. Inside the mattress and blankets were kept and, as they were close by the fire, they were always nice and warm. I loved to sleep in the settle. The big advantage of sleeping in the settle was, if rakers (visitors) were in, I would get staying up until they went home because it could not be opened out until they left.

Before the rakers would arrive the Rosary would be said. Sometimes the rakers would arrive in the middle of the Rosary so they would kneel down and join in the prayers. I loved to sit and listen to the old men telling their stories. Some of these men would have been away working in England or Scotland and had good stories to tell. A good number of the stories would have been made up and most of them were ghost stories or fairy tales. One man who lived next door, his name was Jimmy Gillespie, had been to America and his stories were very interesting and nobody could contradict him because no one knew if they were true or not.

When everyone left Aunt Katie would open up the settle and lay out the mattress and blankets. Pyjamas were not used much then, boys of my age just slept in their shirt. When I got into the bed Dim would start to rake the fire. Raking the fire was a very important job and he was good at it. The fire was the only heating they had, their central heating if you like.

The fire was never allowed to go out, it burned night and day and I suppose you could say it smouldered during the night. To make this happen Dim would rake all the good red coals and ashes out to the side of the hearth. Then he would build some damp turf at the back, which were taken in earlier for that purpose. The red coals were then built up against the damp turf and these were surrounded by more damp turf. Then the whole thing was covered with ashes. The remainder of the ashes were swept up and put on top. The last thing Dim did was to make the sign of the cross over the fire with the tongs. He then sprinkled holy water all around the kitchen and on me as well, before he went to bed.

It was lovely to lie there in my nice warm bed and watch this performance and by the time he had finished I was almost asleep. As Dim left the kitchen he blew out the old single burner lamp that sat on the table. I was left with the little red glow of the Sacred Heart lamp, which hung above me on the wall and it seem to make big shadows across the flag floor. Mostly I went to sleep almost immediately but some times I would lie there and listen to the crickets.

There were crickets in every house then and especially where there was a hearth fire. They loved the heat and they could hide and make their nests in the old lime walls. They did not appear much while people were sitting around the fire. When everyone was in bed they would appear. They would jump around the fire and down on the floor. I remember being afraid that they might jump into the settle as they could jump very high. There was no harm in them, they would not bite or anything, but it just felt a bit creepy. They were very fond of wool and would eat holes in socks that were hung on the crane to dry.

Crickets could be very noisy, especially if there was rain coming. They were known for being good weather guides. If a storm was coming they would stay in the walls and they would not make a sound. When thunder was approaching they would come out but would be very quiet. In frosty weather they kept very close to the fire and you would even see some of them jumping through the ashes. But most of all they loved the heat, the hotter the stones behind the fire, the louder they chirped.

The indoor life of the crickets ended with the putting in of ranges and the renovation of fireplaces. It is a funny thing that, to my knowledge, no one thought it worth their while to do anything to save the cricket. Big efforts were made to save the corncrake and the barn owl and other wildlife but no one seemed to care about the old cricket.

I had not seen a cricket since those years until I went to America in 1980. As I got out of the car at my sister's house I could not believe the noise I was hearing, thousands of crickets. The next day I did not stop looking until I found one. When I did I could see that it was almost the same as the ones that had jumped around the fireplaces in Ireland, just not as brown.

Old Jimmy Gillespie told me a story about why they have so many crickets in America. Jimmy said that when people were going to America they put a cricket into their trunk for good luck and when they arrived, the cricket got free and as the climate was warm, they survived and multiplied. So now you know why they have so many crickets in America – they all emigrated from Ireland!

Back at Aunt Katie's house, Dim was an early riser. In the summer time he would be up about seven o'clock when the first job was to get the fire going. By now the damp turf he had put at the back and sides was burning nicely. So he raked them all out again and put nice dry turf at the back with the coals built against them and more turf around the sides. The kettle was hung on the crook and, in no time, the fire was blazing up around it. By that time I was up and dressed and Dim and myself would go out to feed the cattle. When we returned the kettle was boiled and Aunt Katie had the breakfast ready.

The breakfast usually consisted of porridge and a good big teapot of strong tea and as much scone bread and homemade butter as we could eat. With a good breakfast inside us it was out to the byre to milk the cows and then to all the other jobs that had to be done around the farm.

Paddy was the only cousin I had on my father's side and as he was growing up he spent a lot of time about our house in Derryart; he and Nora and Hugh were around the same age. Paddy married Mary Brogan from Dunfanaghy and they now have four of a family and they still live in Umerafad.

Chapter 5 - The Poultry Station and other Farming

When small grants became available for poultry houses, in about 1945, my mother applied for and received one of these grants. The grant was for a poultry station so two hen houses had to be built. The first house, for laying hens, was reconstructed from an old building and was done by the Wilkins from Magheroarty.

A second house was built some time later for young chickens, they were called pullets. This house was built by Dinny Harkin (Frank) and Ritchie Doherty – Dinny did the building and Ritchie did the timberwork. I attended Dinny at the building, putting stones up on the scaffold and mixing the cement. Dinny had his own way of doing things. Plumb rules were not high on his list of priorities. He used to make one with a piece of timber with a ball of lead hanging on a length of string. When this was held against the wall if the ball fell into the hole in the timber, then it was plumb. Most of the time he judged it by eye and if he could not find the plumb ball, he dropped a spit down the wall, and if it did not hit any of the stones on its way down, then he would say "It's near enough."

My mother was a very hard working and ambitious woman. She and my father worked as a perfect team. He worked in Scotland to earn the badly needed money and she invested it in a good business at home. The breed of hens we kept was White Winedots, which were very big, pure white hens and the roosters were game birds. A netting wire fence ten foot high had to be erected to keep them in. If any stranger went into the enclosure the roosters would attack them. The three roosters had to be replaced every year and I remember one year the three new young roosters arrived in a box, each one in its own compartment. As usual, it was my job to clean out the henhouse. The job had to be well done when the new "cockerels" arrived, as the "poultry mistress" would come around to inspect the house.

One of the old roosters approached the box and started to pick at one of the young ones through the wire. The young one became aggressive and broke out of the box so the two of them started to fight. I thought this was great fun so I let them fight for a while. Then it got out of hand, and the two of them were covered in blood. In my efforts to stop them, I started to wield a big stick and hit one of them on the head. With all the blood I could not see which of them it was.

To my horror, I discovered it was the young one that was lying on the ground with not a move in it. On further examination I found it was dead. What was I to do now? My instinct to save my own skin clicked in to motion so a plan was devised. Each bird had special rings on their legs giving information as to their age etc. It was a simple job of changing the rings. I told my mother that they had a fight and that the old one got killed. My mother did not think much of it as fighting between the roosters was common. Anyway, the old boy was lucky; he got another year to enjoy himself!

The hens were pure bred and their eggs were for hatching. People who wanted eggs for setting would come to my mother and buy the eggs. She had an incubator for hatching eggs and would sell the birds when hatched. Any eggs that were not sold for hatching would be sold to the shop and the government paid a subsidy for them.

The poultry business was a success and was profitable. Things in general on the farm began to recover and as a result, my father was able to stay at home. I often think on those days and how our parents had to work so hard to rear a family of five without any luxury or much comfort for themselves.

My father was nineteen years older than my mother. That difference in age never seemed to affect their relationship, I think this was mainly because my father was always very young at heart and an active man who loved to dance and play music. He would tell stories about the time he was in the County Down. In fact he was always telling stories about the County Down, so much so that someone gave him the nickname "The County Down." He also had another nickname, "The Candy Man", because he used to sing a song of the same name.

My memories of my parents include the two of them dancing around the kitchen when there would be a crowd gathered in, and that was quite often. My father danced the hornpipe and could do so until a short time before his death at the age of eighty-six in 1976. When he went to Scotland to make money to rear the family and to help set up the poultry station he was about fifty-five years of age which was a good age to be to work at jobs like farming and building a hydro dam in Pitlochry. We were lucky as a family that my father had only to spend about ten years working in Scotland as some children only saw their father once a year until they were adults.

After leaving school I worked on the farm along with my father and my brother John. We had twenty-one acres of arable land and about ten of rough ground. Our farm was considered to be a good farm and was big compared with other farms in the area. The land was reasonably flat, dry and with good deep soil. The main crop in those years was potatoes, with the main varieties being Aran Banner and Kerr's Pinks. Kerr's Pinks were the top potato for table use then, as they are today and the Aran Banner was planted for seed for export.

Around the Creeslough area the land was very suitable for potatoes and, as I mentioned earlier, Creeslough can boast of holding the world record for growing the biggest crop of potatoes, thirty-four tons to the acre.

The big problem working at home on a farm was getting pocket money. People were self sufficient and never wanted for food, but money was very scarce. I am sure there were times when there was no money on hand in the house and, of course, bank accounts were unheard of. Money was not often needed by a young teenager but the most important time was when the pictures would come to the "wee hall" in Faugher or the Creeslough hall.

The fair day was another time when it was nice to have your own money but, the biggest day of them all was the sports in Portnablagh which was held on August Monday each year. I remember starting to save money as early as May. There were always people home on holiday at the time of the fair who would pay a visit and it was very important to be nice to them and be very mannerly as you had a good chance of getting sixpence or a shilling when they were leaving.

That was the time when many young people learned the skills of making money and how to run a business. It was good training on how to exist on little money and it also made a person thrifty. Discovering ways of turning things to your advantage gave a person a "nose" for business.

One day a man called with my mother, he said he was from the Irish Press newspaper and was told to call here by Brian Mc Ginley, who was manager of the Creeslough Co-Op at the time. He asked if I would be interested in selling the Sunday Press at the chapel gate on a Sunday after Mass. My mother asked me if I would like to do the job and, of course, I jumped at the opportunity. So every Sunday morning the Irish Press van would drop the papers at the door and if it was a wet morning I would get up early and take them in.

After Mass I would get my bundle of papers under my arm and, as I wore a big coat with great big pockets in it, it was easy for people to drop the money in. The price of the paper was three pence, which was a big bronze nine-cornered coin. My customers would pull the paper from under my arm and put the money in my pocket and take change if they needed to. I have to say I was never down any money.

I sold one hundred and twenty papers every Sunday, which amounted to one pound ten shillings (about €1.90 today) and the profit I had was seven shillings and sixpence (about 50 cent today). That was good money for a young fellow of fourteen at that time, especially as it did not take long to do the job.

Another way of making some money was with rabbits. There were thousands of rabbits in every part of the country. That reminds me of the man who said, "I was going to work one morning and as I passed a field I counted a million rabbits and then I lost count." There were a number of ways of catching them but the main method was the trap and snare. The traps would be set just before dark in a place where the rabbits would be known to frequent. They would have to be camouflaged with clay and grass. The snare would be placed on the paths where the rabbits would run, with a little stick holding up the wire.

Then, before bed time, when the rakers would be leaving, the traps and snares would be checked and any rabbits that were caught were taken out and both were set again. It was important to take the caught rabbits in at bedtime as dogs might eat them.

There was nothing as nice as getting up just at dawn on a sunny autumn morning and going across the fields to check the traps and snares. At that time of year, all the whins and bushes and the stubble fields were completely draped with spider's webs. The dew sparkled in the first rays of sunlight on the webs.

It was very exciting to see how many rabbits were caught, as each one represented one shilling or maybe one and six if the prices were good. We mostly sold them to Mary Ann Harkin in Creeslough. Mary Ann would examine them to see if they were damaged in any way. She would catch the rabbit by the hind legs, holding it out straight and if the backbone was broken it would bend in the middle. Rabbits that were caught by a dog might have their backbone broken and that would reduce the price. But we had a remedy for that. We would get a spoke from an old bicycle wheel and shove it up along the backbone, then when Mary Ann held it up it would pass the test.

"Lamping" and shooting were other ways of getting rabbits. Lamping was done at night time with a very bright light. When the light was shone at the rabbit he became dazzled and it was easy for the dogs to catch it. There were many types of lights used for the job. Before the battery lamps, there were carbide lamps. The light from this type of lamp was produced by water dripping from a little tank into a container of carbide, producing a gas, which was piped to a burner where the flame burned. A very powerful reflector and magnifying glass made the light very bright.

Shooting was another method of catching rabbits but this method had a number of disadvantages. The rabbit would be badly damaged and the buyers did not like the grains of shot that would be in the flesh. Another draw back with the gun was that when you shot one rabbit the rest ran away and did not return for a long time.

My next-door neighbour, Ritchie Doherty, was a great man for inventing things. Ritchie made a contraption one time for lamping rabbits. It was part of the frame of a bicycle with one wheel on it, which had a dynamo. Now this frame was strapped onto Ritchie's back, with the pedals out in front of him, and a lamp with a strong bulb in it. The pedals were then turned by hand which turned the wheel with the dynamo. A very bright light was produced. However after a few nights carrying this monstrosity over hill and dell, it was given up as a bad job. Then a big long torch with six batteries in it became available. There was a very powerful light from it, which was adjustable and easy carried, and it did the job much better.

I mentioned this man at the beginning of the book, Barney Diver, who travelled around working for his keep on any farm who needed him, and who used to stay in our house for long periods. He was an expert at catching rabbits, especially shooting them. Barney used to go out in the moonlight with the shotgun to shoot rabbits but then he developed an invention for shooting on dark nights. He mounted a six-battery lamp on the barrel of the gun and when he shone it on the rabbit, all he had to do was pull the trigger. Barney would stay about our house during the winter and early spring and then he would get restless and move on.

Barney was a great man for inventions and using his initiative. Dogs were a big problem around a hen house, especially stray dogs, and mind you there were plenty of those. In the henhouse door there was a small door to allow the hens in and out. Inside the henhouse there were nests all around the walls and the dog could easily lift one of the eggs from the nests. Barney used to take the grains from the shotgun cartridges and replace it with rice or coarse salt. He would lie in waiting for the dog and when it was half way in the little door with just his hind end out, he would let him have the rice or the salt in the posterior. This would not do him any harm or wound him but it gave him a terrible fright.

The dog would then go into a mad panic and would come back out through the little door and as he made his get-a-way, Barney would let him have another shot in the rear. That dog would not come back for a long time but, sure enough, in time he would forget his unfortunate experience and come back to try it again.

Another deterrent to the dog was an eggshell with mustard in it. When the unsuspecting dog reached into the nest and lifted the mustard filled egg with his mouth and proceeded to eat it, you can imagine the effect it had on his throat. He would head for the nearest water hole and drink as much water as he could. Again this unpleasantness would keep him away from eggs, for a while at least.

Barney also had some very funny sayings, which he usually made up himself. One of his famous statements after eating a good meal was, "It was most obnoxious to my devisious tasture." Of course that meant it was very good and tasty. I have very fond memories of Barney and I kept in touch with him until he died. Barney spent the last twenty years of his life in St. Connals hospital in Letterkenny where his talents were put to good use in fixing clocks and watches. He had his own workshop, and felt very important. He was very happy there and was very well thought of by the doctors and staff. Barney died in 1980 and was taken back to be buried in his beloved Doe.

Chapter 6 - The Harvest

The work on the farm was tough but there were some good times. I always loved the harvest time. We would usually have about four or five acres of corn which would produce about eight to ten stacks. In the earlier years the horses and reaping rachine did the cutting of the corn but some years, when the weather was very bad and the fields would become wet, the corn would have to be cut with the scythe. One good man with the scythe and two men lifting after him could cut one acre in a day. Before the reaper was brought into the field one "sward" – a sward is the stalks of corn cut by the scythe and left lying to be lifted and tied into a sheaf – had to be cut around it with the scythe. This was called "opening the field."

The men in those days were so particular they would not allow any corn to be trampled by the horses and reaper. This job was usually done in the evenings a few days before the cutting proper would start. It was our job as children to "hold the rod" which was not a very popular job. A straight rod would be cut from the hedge, preferably from a sallow bush, and it then was held against the stalks of corn to keep it from falling over on the scythe blade as it was been cut. As you held the rod against the corn, you had to walk backwards along the edge of the field which had a number of hazards.

One big problem was the briars that would grow out from the side of the field and wind their way into the corn and, as you reversed back along the corn, your legs got torn on the briars. Another hazard was the midges and I used to think that my father must have had skin like leather because the midges never seemed to bother him. It was very difficult to keep the rod on the corn and keep the midges from your face at the same time. When you finally got in from the field as it was just getting dark you were a sorry sight with a red face from the midges and the backs of your legs all scrapped and bleeding from the briars.

In the year 1949 our neighbour, Mick McGarvey, got a new tractor. That was the end of the horses and reaper. It was a custom then for two farmers to work together, which was locally known as "working in means." I still remember the day Mick came with the new tractor, it was a Ford Ferguson, which ran on petrol. As far as I can remember Manus Gallagher from Creeslough who worked in McMahon of Milford where the tractor was bought, drove the tractor home for Mick. Mick then returned with Manus leaving him back in Creeslough, and on his return, John and myself was waiting to see him come down the road with the new tractor. He stopped with us and, as it was the first time we were close to a tractor, we were looking all around it with great excitement. It was also Mick's first time to drive a tractor, or any mechanical propelled vehicle as the only lesson he had was leaving Manus back in Creeslough which was a distance of three miles. I think he was getting nervous of us coming too close to the machine when he said, "Stand back, for you wouldn't know when this thing would take off."

The old reaper was modified to suit the tractor. The long shaft, which the horses used to pull the reaper along, was cut and an iron hitch put on to it to enable the tractor to pull it instead. All sorts of machinery could be used with the tractor. One very useful piece of equipment was the trailer, and it made the taking in of the corn from the field fast and easy.

In good harvest weather the cutting and saving of the corn was very pleasant. Work would start about nine o'clock in the morning after the cattle were fed and put out to the field. Dinner was at half past twelve and by then everyone was ready for a good feed.

I remember watching the house to see some of the women out washing the potatoes; you knew then that it would only be about an hour until the dinner was ready. In those days most households would have a half-barrel of herring salted and a pig cured and hung.

During the harvest time, dinner would mostly be herring, which meant you would be very thirsty for the rest of the day. Of course there could also be bacon, turnips and cabbage, chicken, or maybe rabbit. People might not have had much money in those days, but there was never a shortage of food, as the farmers were self-sufficient.

The tea in the evening was the most enjoyable meal of the day. Again, the young ones of us would keep a watch on the house to see the appearance of my mother with the big basket. Sometimes, if some of the girls were helping with the lifting of the corn, they would go to the house and help to prepare and carry the food to the field. They would arrive with two big baskets of bread with homemade butter and jam on it. As there would be plenty of blackberries at that time of year, it would usually be blackberry jam. They would have two kettles of tea with milk and plenty of sugar in it. Everyone took sugar in those days, no word of slimming. We would all make seats for ourselves with sheaves of corn and the feast would begin.

After the tea was over and the men had their smoke, the "stooking" of the sheaves would start. A stook was four sheaves stood together and tied at the top with a band of straw. During that time the young ones of us who would be having a smoke on the sly, would make an excuse to leave the field. The work would usually stop about seven o'clock. Then the cows would be put in to the byre, milked and fed for the night. Hens, ducks, horses and any other animals would be fed and closed in for the night. Everyone then gathered in to the house and the supper was made.

After the supper, the fire would be built up with more turf and the family gathered around and the day's work was talked about. At that time of year the nights would be long and the odd "rakers" might drop in for a chat. After discussing how many acres of corn the neighbours had and how many stacks they would have, the state of the country, and indeed the world, would be talked about. We got a radio about that time and the young ones of us would try to listen to Radio Luxembourg while the older ones talked. There was no such thing then as a radio in the bedroom. One of the hit songs I remember at that time was "Dear Hearts and Gentle People."

Rakers played a big part in the life of the community. In other parts of Donegal it was known as "ceilidhing" but it had the same meaning. People would gather into houses and sit and talk and that was where most people learned the art of storytelling. Ghost stories and fairytales were a big part of the folklore, and many a young person went home running for fear of the ghosts and the fairies that they heard stories told about.

If it had been a good harvest with nice dry weather, the corn would be ready for building in about two weeks. A good corn stack was always built in a certain way and was started by the cutting of the whins for the foundation of the stack. This was known as "the stile." The whins were built around in a circle with the jagged end facing out which served to keep the sheaves of corn off the ground. A good stile could also keep the rats out of the stack. When they were pressed together with the weight of the stack, the jags were so close that the rat could not make his way in. The stack was built in circle with the heads of the sheaves in towards the centre of the stack. The bottom part of the stack was called the "butt."

When the stack was built the butt was "spaded" and this was done with a spade being shoved in through the stalks of the corn. This procedure was done to tighten the butt and make it harder for a rat to penetrate it. It also kept the geese from pulling straws from the stack. The last job to be done to the stack was the thatching which was done with rushes and, finally, the stack was roped with straw ropes to keep it secure and upright. Now that the corn was saved and in the haggard, the potatoes were the next job.

We always dug the potatoes "In Means" – working with another farmer and sharing the horses and tools – with my grandfather Big Jim. The weather could be a problem when digging the potatoes. It was much colder at that time of year than it was at the cutting of the corn. Going out to the field on a cold November morning with the odd hail shower and having to pick those potatoes out of the mucky clay was not very pleasant. But then there were some good days with the sun shining and the clay nice and dry, which made it a much more pleasant experience.

We usually started digging with Big Jim in Ballymore. He always drove the horses and digger. It was much easier gathering the potatoes after the digger than the plough as the digger scattered the drill, but the plough only split it down the middle so you had to pull the drill apart with your hands. The potato digging in Ballymore would take about two weeks if the weather was good.

We would dig Dinny Harkin's (Frank) potatoes as well. We worked in pairs, the young ones on the out side to get the scattered potatoes. Dinny was always great crack to be paired with as he kept telling stories and, as I said before, he was never very particular and if the job was reasonably well done Dinny would make his usual statement, "It'll do rightly." He told a story about the first time he went to Glasgow with another neighbour man. They were walking along the banks of the Clyde on a lovely summer evening and a large number of young girls were sitting along the river. Some of them moved down close to the bank and one of them fell in to the river. Dinny said to the man who was along with him "We'd better help that girl," but the man said "Let her lie there, sure you wouldn't know what trick she might be at." We then asked Dinny what happened to the girl, was she drowned? Dinny said, "Well, do you know what happened, a manly fellow jumped in and pulled her out."

Another job that was very laborious was the cutting and saving of the turf. The turf cutting started around the middle of April, depending of course on the weather. The saving and taking the turf out of the bog could last until July and maybe August.

The turf bank, as it was called, had to be pared. This was a tough job and was done with a spade. The top sod, which consisted of a layer of heather and half dried peat, had to be dug off and placed in what was known as the 'hole of the bank', that was the low ground where the turf had been cut off the year previous. It was very important that the sod was placed on this low ground as this kept the bog growing and in years later, would produce turf again.

There was a special spade for cutting the turf which was like an ordinary spade, only it was straight and had a wing out on one side, this wing shaped the turf. The man cutting the turf would cut two turf which were then placed on the high ground by the man standing in the hole. Depending how deep the bog was, there could be three turf deep cut along the bank.

If the weather was good, the turf would be ready for turning in a week at which time they would be stood up in groups of 8 or 10. This was known as 'footing'. In Donegal it was mostly called 'fitting' or 'rickling', and allowed the wind to blow through and dry the turf. The sods of turf were then ready for taking out to the side of the nearest road and there were a number of ways of doing this. One way was to carry them in bags on your back, then, there was the donkey and creels and the donkey and cart and of course if the bog was dry enough, in later years they were loaded on to a tractor. That was the main part of the work done; all that remained was to take the turf home.

The most memorable part of working in the bog was having the tea. The first job after arriving in the bog was to light a fire which was important as the fire had to be burning well when it came to putting on the kettle and the saucepan to boil the eggs. The next job was to dig a hole into the side of the bank and the butter and milk was placed in it to keep the butter from melting or the milk from going sour. As the breakfast would have been taken about seven o'clock and seven miles travelled on a bicycle, you would be well ready for food by mid-day. A white tablecloth would be laid down and big scones of wheaten and raisin bread would be sliced and piled high in the middle of the cloth. Eggs were boiled and handed around to everyone. By this time the big kettle of strong tea was brewed and poured into the mugs. The container of home made butter was then taken out of the "cooler" and then the feast would begin.

Taking the turf home in those years was a huge task, as it had to be done by horse and cart and was very time consuming and labour intensive. When I was a child I remember being told the night before that we were going to the bog in the morning for a load of turf. We would be awakened at six o' clock in the morning and John and me would go out and feed the horse and get the cart ready for the journey.

After a good breakfast my father would take the scythe and cut a sheaf of rye in the field that was grown mainly for this reason, as it was considered to be good feeding for the horse. Along with some corn for the horse and food for ourselves, and a few bottles of water for drinking, we were all ready for the road. A big bag of straw was filled and put into the cart for sitting on. The front board of the cribs would be placed across the cart under the side cribs at the front and this was where the driver sat; a bit like a dickey – a driver's seat in a carriage. We would be ready for the road shortly after seven o'clock.

The place where we cut our turf in Derryfad was 6 miles away and the journey taking the short cut went down Duntally and over Killoughcarron through Drimeasson and ending up in Derryfad, just above Glen Lough.

As we travelled along, the noise from the irons on the wheels was deafening as they crunched over the gravel road and hopped off the many big stones that were strewn on the road. The horse would stop – without being directed – at a number of watering holes along the way. When the cart stopped it seemed as if the whole world came to a stand still as the noise from the wheels and the jumping of the cart stopped, and you could hear the birds singing. When we arrived at the bog the horse needed a rest and some food and we also needed to stretch ourselves and have some food and drink. Then the horse was yoked into the cart again and the turf were thrown into it.

When the cribs were full my father would build turf around bringing it up to a round top. Then it was back to the road again on the way for home. On the return journey we had to walk because there was no room in the cart and the load of turf was heavy enough for the poor horse. The journey home had to be the long way, 7 miles, because the short road was too hilly. It would be around mid-day when we got home. After a good meal and a change of horse, it was back on the road again and the whole thing was repeated for another time. This procedure was repeated many times during the summer months until all the turf were taken home. This method was stopped in the early 50s when lorries became available to the small farming community.

At the end of the 1940s and early 1950s I have very pleasant memories of going to my Aunt Rose in Magherablade, not far from Doe Castle, to take the donkey and cart up to Drimeasson bog in the morning to take out turf. I would usually go there on a Sunday evening to be there on Monday morning early, to go to the bog. My Aunt Rose was married to Andy Boyle and they had a son and daughter, Ann and Neil. They lived in a beautiful place not far from the sea just looking across at Ards Friary. It was so peaceful there on a summer evening, nothing to be heard but the call of the curlew. Andy was a very good worker and was very particular in the way he did things around the farm. In the evenings when I came home from the bog, after getting a good dinner, I would go out with Andy to help him with putting cows out to the field after milking. Andy was an early riser and for that reason it was always early to bed. I can remember going to bed on a lovely summer evening about 10.30 with the sun setting in the west, which was just the view from my window upstairs in a little room at the back of the house. The only sound to be heard was the big clock striking down in the kitchen and, of course, the curlew calling at the bottom of the fields as the tide came in.

It was a pleasant run on a July morning, along by Doe Castle over the rampart at Cashel and along by the sea to the Lackagh, and then going up the hill towards Drimeasson and arriving at Derryfad bog. The donkey cart did not make as much noise as the horse cart on the road and the donkey could trot along faster than the horse. Andy would have time to milk the cows after I left and be in the bog on his bicycle when I arrived. After a long hot day loading and emptying the cart it was back the same journey again, ready for a wash and a good meal. Aunt Rose always had some fun and stories before retiring for a well earned sleep – the clock was not heard that night. There were times during the summer months in those years when I would stay with Aunt Rose and Andy for a week, going to the bog every day with the donkey cart.

The farm work continued much the same up until the mid 1950's. At that stage there was more work to be found with Donegal County Council, the Forestry and other employers. On the music scene, the big hits of the time that I remember were "The Little White Cloud that Cried" by Johnny Ray in 1951, "Cold Cold Heart" by Hank Williams also in 1951 and "Jambalaya" 1952 and "Walking my Baby Back Home" by Nat "King" Cole in 1952.

I joined the F.C.A. in1952. These initials stand for "Forca Cosanta Aitiúil" meaning Local Defence Force. There was a large number of members in the Creeslough area at the time and Master Joe Doherty, Creeslough, was the captain in charge. The training was very good and Joe took his job very seriously. We trained every Tuesday night in the Creeslough Hall and one Sunday in the month we had a "field day." That was a day's training out through the fields and roads and sometimes we trained at night.

The training we received with the FCA was very good and I must say I learned skills that I found very useful throughout my life. We were taught first aid, self-defence and a lot of discipline, which is good for any young fellow. Every year we went to summer camp in Finner army barracks near Bundoran for two weeks training. For those two weeks we got a taste of what the regular army was like.

One of the highlights of going to Finner was going to Bundoran at night to the dances in the Astoria ballroom. One of the big hits at the dances then was the tango and the big hit tune was "Cherry Pink and Apple blossom White", played by Eddie Calvert on his golden trumpet. We did a lot of guard's of honour for various people from government ministers to bishops. I was involved in three guards of honour for President Sean T. O'Kelly.

Chapter 7 – Public Work

In 1953 I went to work with Donegal County Council and we were working at Ned's Rock in Faugher, near Portnablagh, quarrying stone. One day we were sitting on top of a pile of stone having our lunch, which consisted of good strong tea in black tins that was boiled on the fire, eating homemade scone bread and jam. Very few men would have sandwiches or any type of meat on their bread.

As we sat there the men were complaining about the type of work we had to do and how we had to sit on stones drinking tea from black tins. Just then a large car passed by and some of the men said "Look at that man in his big car; he doesn't have to work in these conditions." As if the man in the car heard what was said, the car stopped and reversed back. It came to a halt right in front of where we were sitting. It was the biggest car that I had ever seen; it was long and black with a big door on the side of it.

The front door opened and the driver got out, the door on the back started to slide back and a ramp came out which rested on the ground. Down the ramp came a big man sitting in a wheel chair and he said to the driver "Push me over to the men until I talk to them." The driver pushed him over and he said to us "Sorry to be intruding on you while you are having your meal, but I always like to talk to working men like yourselves. My name is Singer, you know the people who make the sewing machines," he said "And this is a special car built by Rolls Royce and Singer. I have everything I want, all the money I will ever need, but I can not walk one step and will have to sit in this wheel chair for the rest of my life. You might be wondering why I stopped to tell you that story, but when I see men along the road doing manual work, I wonder if they realize how fortunate they are to be able to do it?"

With that his driver wheeled him back into the car and he was gone. It was five minutes before anyone spoke and then one of the jokers said, "He would have made a good enough ganger, sure they don't work anyway, they might as well be sitting in a wheel chair."

For the next year I worked at various jobs from building walls, cleaning water tables and towards the end of the year I went to work at the stone crusher at Sculldarragh in Knocknafaugher. Paddy McGinley from Kilmacloo was the foreman there and Dan McGinley (Peter), Marble Hill, was in charge of the stone crusher and the steam engine. Sometimes a number of men would be sent from the quarry to work at other jobs – it might be helping with tarring or other road works.

One time Charles John Coll, Andrew Coll, Willie Coll and myself were sent to the Ards Road to do some tarring. It was the road from the junction at the bottom of the waterfall bray, to Barr's gate. When you went through Barr's gate, you were in the Ards Friary grounds. This was the first time this part of the road was tarred. Eddie Lafferty was the ganger man. John Joe Langan was driving the lorry and his brother Packie was working there also. The first job that had to be done was what was known as mud rolling. Two-inch stones were scattered on the road and clay was spread over the top of them. Barrels of water were taken by the lorry and emptied out on the clay and the clay and the water was brushed in through the stone. Eddie used to shout to us, "Make slurry of it, boys." This was the foundation for the tar and chips. Then the big steamroller and the tarring machine arrived and at this stage the whole operation went into overdrive. Charles John Coll used to say that the smell of the steam and tar had an effect on everyone and it made them unreasonable.

Thinking back on it now, I wonder how Eddie Lafferty kept his sanity. The four of us who came down from the quarry knew every trick in the book to make things difficult for the people in charge. Eddie would say, "I don't know what crime I committed to be punished like this, the sooner the four of you go back to the quarry where there is nothing to break only stones, the better for everyone." But, even with all the acting, we still did a good job. After that it was back to Sculldarragh. I worked there until January 1954 when I went to work in Ards Forest.

The forest was a much more pleasant place to work. I've always had a flair for working with wood so it suited me much better than working with the council. There were about forty men working there at the time. There wasn't a ganger as such, just one of the workmen who filled in the book and kept the time sheet. The boss was Joe Conway who lived in Creeslough and married a local girl, Nell Ferry of Ferry's pub in Creeslough. The older men who worked in the forest, some of whom had been working there since 1930, were all a dedicated bunch of men. These men did their job to perfection, and most of the time they were left to do the work without supervision.

The work was tough and the day long, from eight in the morning till six in the evening, with one break. Trees were felled with crosscut saws and axes and were then pulled down by hand and the branches cut off them. The trees, which were about forty feet long, were hoisted on the backs of two men and carried to the edge of the forest, which could be as far as one hundred and fifty yards.

Despite all the hard work, the young ones in the group could always find something to entertain ourselves. We often got into trouble when the boss turned up unexpectedly and caught us doing Elvis or Buddy Holly impressions, using the axe as a guitar. We were a constant annoyance to the more mature men who just wanted to get on with the job.

One day an inspector of some sort came around and announced that all the trees less than six inches in width had to be cut with the axe. For those of us who had plenty of experience handling an axe it was easy enough but for young fellows who had just started, it was very difficult. One day a man from Newtowncunningham came into the forest to buy some timber and, as he stopped his lorry to ask for directions, there was a young fellow who was not long working in the forest cutting a tree with his axe by the side of the road. This young man was hitting around the butt of the tree with his axe but was not having much success in cutting it. The man observed him for a little while and then he said, in his best Newtown accent, "He's a willin wee woochel but he's no takin much oot." That poor unfortunate young fellow had to listen to that "saying" for a long time.

At one stage I was sent to work in Horn Head where the Forestry Commission had taken over some land for planting. Horn Head is a peninsula jutting into Sheephaven Bay and about a five-mile journey from where I was working. The land being planted was known as the sandy hills, 100% sand. The planting had been going on for some years before I went there but without much success. In the summer time it was a heavenly place to work, right on the edge of the sea, with sand all around. I enjoyed many months there working with the Horn Head men who were very relaxed people, a joy to work with and always the best of crack.

The usual gang who worked there were James Dinsmore, Charlie and Bob Campbell from Horn Head along with Frank Herrighty from Ards and myself, and sometimes John Lafferty of Rockhill. James Dinsmore was a big tall man who always suffered from stomach ulcers. His main cure for the ulcers was baking soda. He ate the powder dry every time he took a bout of the stomach pain and that was about every hour. He told me he was taking baking powder for over ten years and he said, "I have as much baking soda taken as would keep the Milford Bakery going."

Chapter 8 - The Forest

On the 31st of January, 1957 I went to work in Ards forest as usual. Little did I realise that it would turn out to be a very unusual day.

The morning was cold with the odd shower and the wind was gusting. We all gathered at the old shed where the tools were kept and, armed with saws and axes, we made our way up the hillside. Our work that day, like every other day, was felling trees in a compartment of Sitka Spruce.

The group of workers consisted of five or six young fellows, with a few older, mostly married men. The uppermost thing on the minds of us young fellows was the dance that night and how we would get there. This was the last Thursday in the month, which meant it was the fair day in Falcarragh and there was always a dance on the fair night.

At around eleven o'clock the wind began to gust strongly and trees were whipped about like sally rods. At twelve o'clock we went for our tea break. When we returned to work, the wind was much stronger and big trees, some of them over one hundred feet high, were crashing to the ground. The only thing we could do was go to a place where there were no high trees. We stayed there until the wind settled, as it was too dangerous to move about. Even during the storm, we still wondered if we might get to the dance.

When the storm settled, we emerged to see that the forest was like a battlefield. Acres of forest were flattened to the ground. Some trees, which had stood the storms of two hundred years, were now lying flat, with a mountain of soil pulled up by their mighty roots. The oldest people around the area said they had never seen anything like the storm that day. We never did make it to the dance that evening.

The next week was spent clearing roads and pathways through the forest. Then came the task of assessing the extensive damage and counting the number of trees tumbled or damaged by the massive storm that day. Looking back on it, I think the winds that day must have been blowing at gale force 8, at least. Suffice to say, I've not experienced another storm like that since.

Those years working in the forest hold great memories for me. It was during that period throughout the 1950's that I did most of my dancing and followed the show bands. Our local hall was, of course, Creeslough Hall. Jim McCaffrey owned the hall and he usually had all the big bands of the time playing there.

"Paddy McCafferty's Band" from Ballybofey was very popular, as was "The Keynotes", and on a Sunday night we used to have "The Glen A Band."

Sunday nights were the nights when I first started to dance. There would be the cinema (the "pictures") in the hall on a Sunday night, which would finish at ten thirty and then the hall would be cleared for the dance. One of my mates at the time was Bernard McGinley who was a nephew of Mrs McCaffrey, Jim's wife. We would help to clear the hall for the dance so then we would get in free. Getting in free was very important as money was very scarce and it was also very important not to have to ask your mother or father for money. You see, there was a bit of strategy used here. The whole problem of getting to a dance arose at the point of asking. And, mind you, asking was necessary even up to the age of seventeen years and, depending on where you were going, maybe older. The Sunday night dance was a good night to start with.

On a Sunday evening after tea I would make it known that I was going to the pictures, this was usually accepted better than if I asked to got to a dance. Another plus on the side of the pictures was the money. Admission was only one shilling and sixpence and one rabbit sold to Mary Ann would pay for that. Then after the film was over the dance started, which was finished by twelve thirty, and as we got in free to the dance that was another one and sixpence saved. Unless you had to leave a girl home from the dance you were home at a reasonable hour.

From 1953 until the early 1960's were my main dancing years. That was the time of Rock and Roll. We did not have the money to buy records, and there were not many places where records were sold, so we just listened to the hit songs on Radio Luxembourg. The big bands around the north west of Ireland at the time were The Clipper Carlton, Sliabh Foy, Melody Aces, Rhythm Boys and many more. We travelled to dance halls in Falcarragh, Gortahork, Derrybeg, Carrigart, Milford, Letterkenny and even as far as Muff and Buncranna.

It is interesting to note some of the popular songs that were hits in the mid to late 1950's. "Your Cheatin' Heart" and "Take these Chains from my Heart" by Hank Williams who also died in that year of 1953. In 1955 there was "Memories are Made of This" sung by Dean Martin; in 1956 "Suddenly there's a Valley" by Jo Stafford, "Singing the Blues" by Guy Mitchell, "I'll Be Home" by Pat Boone and "Just Walking in the Rain" by Johnny Ray were all hits. 1957 heralded "Love Letters in the Sand", "April Love" and" "Remember You're Mine" by Pat Boone. 1958 saw "Sugar Moon" by Pat Boone and in 1959 there was "Cool Water" by Johnny Ray and "He'll Have to Go" by Jim Reaves.

Anyway, back to the storm. What happened that day, the 31st of January 1957 was to change the lives of the people in the Creeslough/Dunfanaghy area. As a result of the trees being blown down, a man by the name of Albert Lykes from Belgium came into the area and bought the trees.

Mr Lykes' foreman came to Creeslough and started putting together a group of workers who would carry out the job of taking the trees from the forest to Ards Pier where they would be shipped to various places as pit props. The foreman's name was Franz Valkenborghs. People around Creeslough were not used to "foreigners" coming into the area so this man was the subject of many a conversation. He was known locally as "The wee Belgian." Little did he realize then that he would meet and marry a local girl, Frances Kelly from Creeslough, and put down roots in the parish that are still here to this day. The name Valkenborghs is now a Creeslough name.

The work was a boon to the area, as many of the men were unemployed at the time. The trees were cut into lengths for pit props and transported to the pier at Ards. Ards was a small pier along an inlet of Sheephaven Bay; surrounded by sandbars, it was like an obstacle course for navigating a boat through. The boats always had to work with the tides, which meant the men had to work night and day to get the boat loaded for the full tide. This work continued for about three years.

At that time Neil Blaney was Minister for local government and was introducing grants for rural areas. Mr. Lykes was on the ball again and secured a grant for a veneer factory on a site where trees had been blown down by the storm. This was in the townland of Cashelmore along the road between Creeslough and Dunfanaghy. As I said, this changed the way of life in this very rural area for the next twenty years. This was previously a small farming countryside, with a lot of emigration; the people who stayed at home worked their small farms, with a few cattle and seed potatoes. They subsidised their income by working with Donegal County Council and with the Forestry Department. Factory work was something they knew nothing about, but they were to learn all about it in the years ahead. The veneer factory officially opened in 1960.

We knew nothing about veneer, and very little about its uses. The big logs started arriving from places as far afield as Africa and the huge machines were set in motion. I remember the first sheet of veneer that came off the big peeler; in fact I still have a piece of it. The peeler worked like a giant pencil sharpener and the sheets that came off the peeler were used for making plywood. Shortly after that, other machines were installed; one was called "a slicer." The logs were steamed in a big pit and when they were soft it was much easier to slice the timber.

Another man came to work in the factory and his name was Franz Van Hoof. He was also Flemish and had been working in Dublin in the pig fattening business. Franz worked as a labourer at the factory and was then promoted to the position of foreman. He was very useful as an interpreter as there were a few Germans at the factory installing machinery. He stayed in our house during his time working in the factory. Franz insisted on being treated as one of the family and called my mother "Mammy", as we all did.

I remember helping him to figure out the setting up of a boiler and steam engine for the factory. During the day the German experts would put in to place different parts of this machine, and would tell Franz how to work it. In turn he had to interpret everything they said and be able to explain it to the other men. This machine was to drive the turbines to make the electricity and produce the steam to soften the timber in the steam pits before it was sliced.

In the factory's hey day sixty workers were employed, men and women. The workers soon learned the skills of factory work, the girls being much more nimble handling the thin sheets of veneer than the men. Before long, the factory was in full production working around the clock, night and day. Over the years the factory changed hands a few times. The demand for veneer in furniture making dropped throughout the 1970's as interior design fashions changed and the factory found it hard to make a profit. A builder's provider store was carried on after the factory closed but it also closed down in about 1984.

Chapter 9 - The Guitar

It was December 1958 and Bridie Gallagher from Ards, Creeslough, was a major singing star. We were all very proud of her. It was something great to have a girl from the parish, famous far and wide and to be able to say that you knew her as a neighbour. Back then we only heard about big stars, or saw them on the big screen in the cinema, so to know our very own celebrity was something special.

I considered myself as a bit of a singer and would sing at house parties and the odd concert, held in the local Creeslough hall. About four years previously, in 1954, I went to a concert where there were two fellows from Derry singing and playing guitars. I had never seen a guitar up close before and I was fascinated with the idea of playing a guitar and singing.

After that I had a keen interest in guitars. I think it must have been about the end of 1956 when I saw a mail order catalogue advertised in a book and sent away for it. The catalogue duly arrived and I was very excited looking at all the pictures of guitars, accordions and all sorts of musical instruments. Of course, I had to keep within a certain price range, as my pay in the forest was only four pounds ten shillings per week. That was considered good pay those days although most of it had to be handed up at home, you were lucky if you got keeping the ten shillings (about 65 cent today.)

Anyway, I chose a guitar from the catalogue. It was a lovely classic model guitar, sunburst red. The price, including a carrying bag, was £16 which was almost four week's wages. I bought it on hire purchase, and the repayments were two pounds per month for ten months. Every evening when I came home from work, I would ask my mother if there was a parcel for me. After about three weeks I came home one evening and, as usual, my mother had the dinner ready. Sitting to my dinner looking around to see if there were any big parcels about, my mother said " Manus Friel left a big long thing for you today off the railway lorry." That ended the dinner, hungry and all as I was.

The next few evenings were spent trying to tune the guitar. I hadn't a clue what the six notes of the strings were. However I could tune a fiddle, so I thought if I tuned the first four strings, the same as the fiddle, I could then work out the tuning for the other two. That did not work out very satisfactorily, but I practised playing every night until I could play a tune. I can still remember it clearly. It was "Hang Down Your Head, Tom Dooly." The next tune was "The Pub With No Beer" which was a big hit in 1957 for Australian singer Slim Dusty.

Luckily I did not learn any more on that tuning, as it was not correct and would have made it very difficult for me to learn properly. In those days there wasn't anyone in the area around Creeslough who owned, or could play a guitar. The nearest person was a man in Letterkenny, twenty miles away; his name was Charlie McGinley. Along with a very good friend of mine, Danny Langan, I borrowed my brother John's car and headed for Letterkenny.

Danny was the best singer of Hank Williams' songs that you could hear anywhere. He and I would sing at local concerts, and of course we thought the guitar would be a big advantage.

Danny and I used to go to dances from Milford to Gortahork to see the show bands. Some bands would invite people to request songs and if they did not know the song you would have to go up on stage and sing it. Danny Langan could always ask them for a song they did not know, usually a Hank Williams song, and then of course to our delight, he would go up and sing it.

Charlie McGinley was a schoolteacher, and a very talented man in music and all kinds of art. He had connections in Creeslough, so that was how I got to know him. As I said, Danny and myself went to see Charlie and, after showing him the guitar I asked him if he could tune it, and within minutes he had it tuned. Charlie said to me, "You will have to get a tutor." I looked at Danny and then looked at Charlie and said, "What is a tutor?" He explained to me that it was a book showing the notes and chords and other techniques used in playing the instrument. For the next few weeks, I practised every night until I could play and sing the "Pub With No Beer." After about a year I became a bit fed up with the guitar as I did not seem to be progressing very well with my playing and I gave it up completely.

Then, a number of years later, a few of us formed a little band and played around the local dance halls, so I started to take an interest in the guitar again. The band never came to very much, but we enjoyed ourselves. As there was no one else around who played a guitar, it was difficult to learn new techniques, or to measure our progress. However, I enjoyed playing and at least I could entertain myself. I am not sure when we formed the first band but I know we had a few trials at it.

We had a good number of band members over the years but the members we had on the famous night in Aranmore Island were, Jimmy Lafferty from Faugher on drums, Jim McFadden from Creenasmare on accordion, James Brogan from Dunfanaghy on fiddle, Arthur Alcorn from Horn Head on accordion and myself on vocals and guitar. We had other formations at other times and they included,

Charles John Coll from Breaghy, Geddy Moore from Doepoint and sometimes Hughie McLaughlin (Anton) from Creeslough. We changed the name of the band a few times but as far as I can remember the name we used the most was "The Sheephaven Dance Band."

Jimmy Lafferty's house was the place we did our practice, which was at least once a week. I do not know how Jimmy's father and mother put up with the racket. We would get together on a Sunday afternoon and start to play and soon the people would start to gather and join in the fun. The house would be full of neighbours and visitors who would be staying in the Portnablagh hotel and other guest houses in the area. The crack would be mighty and the fellows and girls would dance 'round the kitchen and even out on the street. Mary Lafferty would make tea for everyone and we all went home happy.

I think it must have been around 1959 or 1960 when Jimmy and I were appointed promoters. Our job was to go out and get the gigs. There were few phones then so we had to travel around to the different dance hall owners to get bookings. I had a motor bicycle and that was our mode of transport.

The bike was a Java 250 cc with a pillion seat on the back mudguard. That was Jimmy's seat and a shaky enough seat it was because I was a fast driver at the time with not a lot of sense. I remember one Sunday we went around by Carrigart through Cranford and into Milford, calling on the different hall owners. As we went past Cranford, with Jimmy holding on for all his might, we approached a bridge. Walking on the bridge were four elderly women out for a Sunday stroll. The poor women did not know what way to go when they saw this machine coming at them. Luckily enough they scattered to both sides of the bridge and we just flew in between them. I think we must have taken about ten years off their lives. It taught me a lesson and I never went as fast after that.

Our biggest adventure was in Aranmore Island. We were all excited when we got a booking on the island. It was the first time we had got a booking so far away and Aranmore Island seemed like another world.

Some of the members thought we should improve our image and get stands to put in front of the band on stage, like a proper band that would have stands for sheet music. Sheet music was the least of our trouble, but even so we got the stands made with the name of the band on them.

Jim McFadden's brother Danny had a car and he drove us over to Burtonport to get the boat into the island. There were six of us and all the gear in a Hillman car. When we got to the pier at Burtonport there was a lot of people standing on the pier waiting for the boat. When the boat arrived, it was a half-decker and everyone started to board. We were not sure what to do, as there seemed to be more people than the boat could take.

The next thing we heard was the skipper of the boat shouting to the people who were already on the boat to get off as there were too many people aboard. All the people who got off the boat seemed to disappear into the darkness. One man came over to us and told us to wait, that the boat would be back. We had not noticed that a Guard had arrived on the pier and that was the reason why the skipper ordered some of the people off so he would not have to take the Guard. All the people who got off the boat knew the drill and just dispersed into hiding until the boat returned.

The Guard asked us if we were going to get out to the island and we said we did not know, that we thought we might have to go home. It was obvious, even to us, that the whole operation was to make sure that the Guard did not get to the island. He walked around for about twenty minutes and then left. No sooner had he left, than the boat returned as it was waiting out behind a rock until the Guard had left. All of a sudden, people appeared from the darkness and started to board the boat. Two men helped us to load the gear on the boat and soon we were on the high seas for Aranmore.

When we arrived on the island we were met by a man who took us to the dance hall with his tractor and trailer. After putting our instruments on the stage, we were taken to a house for tea. It was about nine o'clock then and we thought we would soon be starting to play. Little did we know about the way things worked on the island and that we would not sing one song before twelve o'clock. We went back to the hall and started to arrange ourselves on stage. The amplification belonged to the hall and it would be safe to say, it was not top of the range. In those days amplifiers were very basic and did not have much power. We had two microphones with one high stand and one short stand. I had to use the high stand for singing into and James Brogan was left with the short one to pick up his fiddle. It was so short that he had to sit on a low stool and stoop down to the microphone. Arthur Alcorn said he was like a man fixing shoes.

The first couple went on the floor to dance at twelve thirty. We played until after three and thought we could stop then, but were told we might as well play away because we could not get off the island until day light. The dance finally finished about six o'clock. After a bit of negotiation we were taken to a house and got some food. Our pay for the night was eleven pounds. Then it was back to the boat and we set sail for the mainland. At home our parents got up in the morning to discover we had not came home. Panic set in and they were thinking of sending out a search party, but all was well and we eventually arrived home safely. We never managed to go back to play in Aranmore but we often talked about our experience. When I think back on those gigs I am sure the music we played must have been very poor but maybe the people did not notice and we certainly enjoyed ourselves.

In 1958 my life took a turn which was not planed but which led me to a new type of life and to a new occupation. On the 6th January 1958, which was then kept as a Church Holiday, John and my mother went to Gweedore to leave Hugh back at school after the Christmas holidays. My youngest brother Hugh was attending a school near Bunbeg to learn the Irish language. As the night approached I started to feel pain in my ankles and knees. The pain got so bad that when I attempted to go up the stairs to go to bed, I had to go on my hands and knees. The following morning my mother came into my room to wake me for work but I was unable to get out of the bed. She asked me what was wrong and I said I had very bad pains in my knees and ankles. The doctor came and told me I had rheumatic pains. He said you will have to stay in bed for two weeks and then you will have to rest for another four weeks.

About that time Bridie Gallagher was starting on a nation wide tour and, as I sang on her shows at a few of the local concerts, I thought I might be in with a chance to do the whole tour with her. This ailment was going to knock that plan on the head. I asked Dr. Coll if he thought I would be ready for the concerts and he said, "Just concentrate on getting better first." It took two months before I was well enough to go back to work and by that time Bridie was well on with her Irish tour. I did have the privilege of singing with her at a few concerts later but never hit the big time like her.

Chapter 10 - Assurance Agent

1958 saw the end of my working life in Ards forest because in March that year I got a job with the New Ireland Assurance Company. That job became vacant because my brother John, who was the representative in the area, took up a job in the Milford/Rathmullen area. When John asked me to apply for the job, I thought it was out of my reach, as I only had national school education, and not too much of that either. Anyway I applied for the job and got it. Mind you, I think there wasn't much competition.

A man arrived one day, his name was Hugh Hone, and he was the superintendent with New Ireland in Letterkenny. Now Hughie, as he was known, was a tall well-dressed, well-built man with a very forceful character and a great pride in himself and in what he did. He took me around the country and introduced me to all the clients and gave me brief lessons on the marking of books and dealing with money. This was all very new to me and a complete change from the work I was used to for the previous six years. With not having had anything to do with books or money my writing and counting skills were very poor.

I found myself being slightly afraid of Hughie as there was so much difference in his and my ability to do the job I was taking on. After all I was just fresh out of "the bushes" and had not handled a book or pen for many years. I was always conscious of making a mistake, but Hughie would say "The man who did not make a mistake never made anything." He was a man I grew to respect, even though he would often "eat the head off me," but it was soon all forgotten.

That year was particularly bad with snow and, even in the month of March, it was still heavy going in places. Most of the area around Creeslough is very hilly, particularly the foothills of Muckish Mountain. Muckish dominates the landscape from Letterkenny to Gweedore and can even be seen as far way as County Antrim.

Back to the snow. Hughie had a Ford Anglia car and it was the only car that could successfully manoeuvre the snowy roads around Derryreel on the north side of Muckish, or Gortnalake on the south side. Every day we set out on these roads, it was like an adventure, and without doubt, Hughie could handle a car on snow and was well aware of that fact. He enjoyed nothing better than the challenge of a road where no one else would travel, and to be told not to try it, as it was too dangerous. You could be sure that's the road he would take.

One day, on our way along the north side of Muckish in the townland of Derryreel, we passed by a man ploughing in a field with two horses. Hughie said, "What the hell is that man doing?" We stopped and there he was, ploughing through the snow, turning over the black earth with hundreds of seagulls following him. The field was so steep he could only plough down the field and had to come up empty.

As we started on our way again, we proceeded down what used to be a very steep hill. I said to Hughie that there seemed to be something wrong, "What could be wrong?" says he as he sped along through the snow, at high speed. "This hill should be a lot steeper than it is," I said and, just as I spoke, we plunged into a snow drift about ten feet deep. We had terrible trouble getting out of the car as the doors were stuck in the snow. After several attempts to reverse the car out of the drift, we had to go back to the man who was ploughing and get him to pull us out with his horses.

The day would pass very quickly working with Hughie as he was always making a joke about something. We had many small winding roads and laneways to negotiate. A common obstacle on these small laneways was a gate made of barbed wire and hazel rods held together with binder twine. This contraption was then tied to a post at the side of the lane with a rope. When we got out of the car and tried to figure out where this fixture opened Hughie would say, "Have you the blueprint for this contraption?" Some houses did not even have wire or hazel just a big whin bush pulled into an opening in the ditch; that was known as a "Slap."

 As the weeks passed I became more familiar with the area and the handling of books and money. The area that I was responsible for stretched from Falcarragh in the northwest, through Dunfanaghy and along the breathtaking cliffs of Horn Head to Portnablagh. The route followed the rugged coast of Sheephaven Bay to the sandy beach of Marble Hill, past Ards Forest right on to Doe Castle that was once the stronghold of McSweeney's and on to Creeslough. Then Northeast to Rosguill, around the Atlantic drive back to Downings and Carrigart, west along the foothills of Muckish to the Calabar river and on to dark Glenveagh and Glenveagh Castle, where once lived the much feared John Adare. The "trail" then headed south towards Treantagh, past the birthplace of Saint Colmcille, and east again through Lagnahoory to Kilmacrennan. It then headed north again through Termon and Barnes over lovely Lough Salt Mountain, through the little picturesque village of Glen, across the Lackagh River and back to Creeslough.

This district had to be travelled by bicycle. In frost, snow and rain I had to cover this territory every four weeks. A few built up areas, which were few and far between at that time, like Dunfanaghy and Creeslough, were collected weekly. I was lucky as John had a car and was in the same business so I could borrow his car on his day off, but most of the time I pushed around on my old single gear bicycle.

Of course there was more to the job than collecting premiums. New insurance policies had to be sold and then there was the general administration that was part of the job. Life assurance was what we dealt with mostly, but we also sold general branch insurance, for property and cars.

In the end of the 1950's and early 1960's money was still very scarce. Things were starting to move a little, with employment in the Creeslough/Dunfanaghy area improving. The forestry employed around forty men. The electricity was being installed, which gave a lot of employment. About thirty people were working at the laying of the water pipe from Lough Agher at the top of Kildarragh to Creeslough. A new school and housing scheme were being built in Creeslough and the road between Ballymore and Drimnaraw, a distance of six miles, was being upgraded.

Up on the hillside at Sculdarragh, Knockfaugher the stone and filling for the road improvements were lifted, employing another fifteen or twenty men. The work at the stone breaker – or "crusher" as we called it – was one of the worst places on earth to have to work. I had worked in it some years previously and I know all about it. The main work was quarrying and breaking the rocks of whinstone with a sledgehammer. The most unpleasant job of all was putting the stone through the crusher. The "crusher" had to be the worst machine that was ever invented. We had to work continually in a cloud of dust, not to mention the deafening crunching of the steal jaws of the crusher. If it were now, people working at such a machine, would be dressed up like space men.

The only way we could get a bit of a break was to "put a spanner in the works", so to speak. This took special planning on the part of us young fellows. One way of doing it was, when one of us was up feeding the stones into the crusher, a wedge-shaped stone was found and dropped into the jaws. Now this would make a crunching noise, but would not be very productive. At that same time one of our allies on the ground would place a small stone on the belt that drove the crusher, which in turn would knock off the belt.

With the task complete, the whole plant would come to a stand still. Now with the wedge-shaped stone well and truly stuck into the jaws, it would take at leaste twenty minutes to get the whole operation going again. By the time that was all done we would have had a rest and a smoke and some of the dust washed from our eyes.

The one nice piece of machinery in the quarry was the big steam engine. Even then as a teenager, I loved to see that big engine with all its brass shining and its massive wheels turning. It always amazed me when I arrived on a Monday morning to see that machine, with every bit of brass and copper shining like new; it was a real work of art. Dan McGinley was the man in charge of it, and he had a lot of pride in it. Although he knew it was going to be covered in dust in a few hours, he would spend hours polishing and shining it.

Dan had a helper who stayed with him known as a flag's man. His name was Mickey and the two stayed in an old wooden caravan on the side of the road. Some times they did not get along very well, they would argue about little things.

One day Dan had to go to Dunfanaghy to get some tools, when he returned the flags man had the tea ready. Sitting into the tea, Dan noticed that Mickey had an egg boiled for himself. Somewhat annoyed, Dan asked why he did not get a boiled egg too.

Mickey replied "There was only the one egg, so what could I do?"
"What could you do?" said Dan, "If I was in your place I would give you the egg,"
"Well, sure that's what I did," said Mickey.

Selling insurance was not an easy job. Most of my clients were farmers, and small farmers at that. People were not used to paying anything weekly or monthly, or the paying of regular bills. The only regular bills they had to pay were the rates and the rent. Not having a fixed income, they did not like to take on a weekly or monthly payment. Another obstacle to selling insurance was that farmers were inclined to calculate everything by how much a wee bullock would make.

Every three months a man would come to work with me in the district. The reason for this operation was twofold – to check the books to see if everything was in order and, more importantly to write new business. One of these men was a Galway man, and his name was Mick McLaughlin. Mick lived in Buncranna and his job description was an assistant superintendent.

Mick was a lovely man with a great sense of humour, who smoked "Mick McQuaid" tobacco and played golf. He would spend three days in the area, mostly canvassing for new business. Many an hour we spent in houses trying to convince some woman to take out a policy on wee Jimmy or Mary for a half-crown a week, or maybe a shilling on the old mother sitting in the corner to pay her funeral expenses. Mick loved to work in the Downings area, around the Atlantic drive, where we could sit and have our lunch in the summer time and then light our pipes and have a smoke.

Sometimes, after spending a good while trying to convince a woman to take out a policy (it was usually women), she would say "I think I will wait till the next time you are around" Mick would whisper to me "We better put on the record again." Jack Fanning was another inspector who would come around. Jack was different from Mick, he was more forceful in selling and, one way or another, he would sell them a policy. Once we were in a house and the woman started to complain about the policy she had out on her mother who had died. She said "By the time my mother died I had paid three times as much as I got." Without blinking an eye Jack said, "Poor woman lived too long."

In every townland there were characters. I remember in some areas it would take all day to get around the houses, as you would have to sit and take tea and listen to these old characters telling their stories. I suppose that was one of the reasons why I gave up the insurance job. I was more interested in the old stories than I was in selling insurance.

There was an old man I called with every month; he lived with two brothers who were most of the time in bed. He baked his own bread and did all the cooking, which he often shared with me. He made the strongest tea that I ever drank anywhere, as they used to say "You could trot a mouse on it."

As you can imagine, this man did not worry too much about hygiene or cleanliness, so when the bread was being prepared, for instance, there could be anything on the table, like a can of paraffin oil and a container of methylated spirits for the Tilly lamp. I have often seen him preparing the dough on the table with the hens standing on it picking the raisins out of the dough and walking across the table, leaving the track of their feet in the flour. There were no colour-coded dishcloths in these houses. Still, nobody died of food poisoning.

The bread was made in what was known as a "pot oven." It hung over the open fire, the lid covered with burning coals from the fire. Before the bread was put in, the oven had to be heated. This was achieved by hanging the oven on the crook over the fire. At the same time the lid would be put upside-down on the hot coals. Now, as often happened to this man, the soot would fall into the oven and, as his sight was not the best, he usually dropped the dough on top of the soot. The soot and dust would gush out as the dough went into the oven.

The pot oven was then hung on the crook over the big turf fire with the lid in place. Hot coals were put on the lid. With the operation complete this old man might put a herring on the lid and cook it while he was waiting for the scone to cook.

One cold winter day I called at the house, as I had done for many years. The door being open as usual, I walked into the kitchen where there was a big fire on the hearth and old Steven was sitting on a stool by the side of the fire. "Come up and sit down," said he. I sat on the other side of the fire on a wee three-legged stool. (The three-legged stool was used on the old flag floor, as the three legs would sit level on the uneven surface).

Steve asked me if I was in a hurry, when I said I wasn't he said he had a surprise for me. He kept looking at the fire but would not tell me why the fire was so big. Then he looked at the clock and said "We'll soon have the feed now." He took the tongs and scattered the big fire. Out rolled a big ball of what looked like concrete, which he broke with the tongs. I was amazed to see in the centre of the ball was a bird, fully cooked with lovely juices running out of it. He said "Now me boy, tuck into that." It was the most succulent and tasty meat I had ever eaten.

He told me it was a moorhen, and he had cooked it by covering it in blue clay, feathers intact, and then the fire was built around it. As it cooked the feathers stuck into the clay and when the clay was broken off the feathers remained in the clay, leaving the bird clean.

Now Steven was an exception, and thankfully there were not too many like him, as far as the cooking was concerned anyway. But he had his own charm and wit and added a certain quality to the countryside, which made it a more interesting place.

Chapter 11 – Rural Electrification

Very few houses had running water, or sewage in the late 1950's. Electric light was the latest mod con and most areas were being connected. The electric light was a much talked about subject. The ESB would not move into an area unless everyone was taking the light. That meant that the townlands had to be canvassed and people encouraged into signing up. There were always people who did not want to take it, let it be for reasons of affordability, or maybe because they were afraid of it.

Many stories were told at wakes, fairs and local gatherings about the supposed dangers of the electric light. One man who had been in England or Scotland for a while used tell of somebody he knew who was killed just switching on a light! The story was told about the man who went to Glasgow to work, when he returned home after six months he said he had got very little sleep. When asked why, he said he couldn't sleep as the light was on all night. Asked why he did not blow it out, he said, "How could I blow it out? It was hanging up in a bottle."

It was thought by some people that St. Colmcille's prophecy had come true, as he was supposed to have said that the day would come when the kettle would boil in the window.

The decision to have the electricity installed in your house took some consideration. First the financial side had to be looked at, as there would be ground rent to pay every two months, plus the cost of the units of electricity that would be used. As I said before, regular payments of a weekly or monthly nature were feared and not taken on if possible.

With the fear of the cost being too much, a lot of houses only installed one bulb in the kitchen and maybe no power socket. One old lady said "It's very handy till I get the tilly lit."

The wiring up of the countryside brought big changes. All kinds of sales men came around selling everything from radios, washing machines, sewing machines and televisions. The first big sales were in radio – old battery sets were replaced by electric sets and the old battery sets were sold on to areas where there was still no electricity.

Around this time I was offered a job selling gas cookers but I was advised not to take it, as it was thought that gas appliances would soon become obsolete. It was also thought that dry batteries would no longer be needed, as electricity would replace the battery. How wrong they were!

Our house was wired for the electric light by Kevin Mc Glynn from Letterkenny; his brother Joe was married to my sister Mary. I helped him to do the job and took particular notice of how it was done. Kevin was a qualified electrician so he did the job the way it was supposed to be done. At that time you did not have to have any qualifications to wire a house so there were a lot of handy men going around wiring houses. I did a bit more study of the subject from books and with that, along with the tuition from Kevin, I started doing the odd house myself.

Over the years I became quite handy at the electrics and wired a good number of houses for neighbours. I always had a flair for anything to do with wires, at the age of about twelve I had wired up a set of lights for a Christmas tree. The lights were made up with old wire I got from Ritchie Doherty with flash lamp bulbs powered by an old dry battery from a radio. They only lasted about fifteen minutes, as the old battery was almost flat. Ritchie was the man who influenced me in that direction in the first place.

Televisions were slow to come to country areas, mainly because there was a very poor signal and so the picture was bad. The first TV I remember, and maybe the first in the parish, was in Samuel Stewart's of Cashelmore. The house would be full of people every night; I don't know how they put up with the intrusion in their home. It was all the talk at wakes, fairs and raking houses, where someone would ask, "Did you go to see the television in Samuel's yet?"

There was one very good salesman, Ned Gallagher; he was originally from Killhill, between Creeslough and Carrigart. He and a man named Joe McDermott had a shop in Letterkenny where they sold sewing machines, radios and other items. They got an agency for televisions and Ned was the main salesman on the road. I often met up with him in houses where I would be collecting insurance premiums and occasionally I helped him to set up a television in some house.

One of his sales approaches was to ask the people of the house if they would keep a TV for him until he was back in that area again, as he had too many of them in the van. He would then tell them they might as well have the use of the set while they were keeping it. Then he would erect the aerials on the chimney and install the TV set. I asked him once why he went to all the trouble of wiring it all up, when he was only leaving it with them for a short period. He looked at me and said "Sure, you know they will never give it up when they have it for a month or six weeks."

As I said earlier I had a motor bicycle, which was my first mechanical mode of transport, but my mother and father did not want me to get a motor bicycle as they were thought to be very dangerous, which they were. Even the man who sold me the bicycle, David McElhinney of McElhinney's garage in Dunfanaghy, was concerned for my safety. David was a lovely man who liked nothing better than to spend a night in some neighbour's house playing the fiddle. Though he was many years older than me, we became life long friends. The motor bicycle I bought from him was about six months old and cost seventy pounds.

Going around the countryside on my motor bicycle was much easier than walking. I thought then that I had all I would ever need. With a good job and a fast motor bicycle, what more could a young man want? Little did I know? When I think back on those times now I realise that, at every milestone of one's life, it was always the same. You thought "This is it now, I'll never want any more," but you do.

It took me less time to get around the district on the motor bicycle, which was important, as some work on the farm still had to be done. My father did most of the farm work but he could not do it all, after all he was sixty-nine years of age. Potatoes, oats, turnips and hay were still grown in those years. Oats of course was called corn – "Cutting the Corn in Creeslough the Day." The pig business was beginning to improve and it was now possible to make a bit of money fattening pigs.

Signing the contract for Creeslough Community Day Centre.

Taking home the turf Derryart brae about 1940

James and Donna's wedding in Ballymore

In Galway 1968 Celebrating 50 years for New Ireland Assurance Co.

For the launch of my first single 1980

Leo and Janet's wedding in Cumbria

Doing a gig with my son Mark in London 2007

Mark and Donna's wedding in Somerset

Charlie Mc Gee's house Derryherriff Creeslough

Mick Brogan's house Carnamaddy

My Father's Brother's Jim and Barney

Opening of Veneer Factory by
Neil Blaney 1960

Old cottage in Murroe Dunfanaghy.

Putting in the corn. My father,
Sister Nora, Brother Hugh and
cousin Paddy Gillespie

Doe Chapel about 1965

Building stack of corn. John, Mick Mc Garvey and myself

Faugher School 1942

John and myself 1954

Hannah and Mary

Aunt Katie's house
Umerafad, Creeslough

My father and mother with Mary, Hannah and Aunt Katie

My father and mother day after their marriage 1929

John Baxter's house Drumeafla

Old Cottage at Killoughcarron Creeslough

Doe Chapel

Our house at Derryart with rose bush

Muckish from Massinass

Launch of my first record "The Maid of Marble Hill" with my neighbour Bridie Gallagher

Corn stacks 1995

Stooks of corn in my field 1994

Old mill grinding stone at the site where they were made in Ards Forest Park

Putting Cross in position on Muckish 2000

Blessing of cross on Muckish 1951.

Blessing of cross on Muckish 2000

Tra-Na-Rosann Atlantic Drive Downings.

Brogans house (The brae) Carnamaddy Creeslough

Muckish from Lough Salt

My great granny Una, Granny Hannah, Grandfather John and my Father with friends 1912

Group at our wedding, Doe Chapel 1965

Our wedding with Fr Deeney and Fr Godfrey, Ards Friary

St John's Church Ballymore

St. Michael's Church Creeslough

Receiving trophy for ballad singing
at Creeslough Féis 1973

Flying the cross to Muckish 2000

Finn, Jamie, Tómas, Orlaith

With Michael and Pat Coyle 1989

Chapter 12 – Keeping Pigs

One day I went to the fair in Letterkenny and bought two pigs. I did not know much about pigs, and the man selling the pigs could see I was a bit "green". He sold me the two smallest pigs in the box. They cost ten pounds for the two.

I put the two pigs in a bag and tied them on the back of the motor bicycle and headed for home. When I got home, my father had a pen made ready in an old hen house, he had it all fixed with straw on the floor. Looking at me and the motorbike he said, "I thought you were getting pigs?" Then he saw movement in the bag tied on the back and realised the pigs were in the bag. "If there's two pigs in that bag," he said "They must be dammed wee."

The two pigs were shivering when we took them out, I suppose from the cold, and they must have been terrified on the back of the motorbike. They disappeared into the straw and did not appear for about two days. Though they were small, they were ready for the factory in three months. I was paid thirty pounds for the two and it cost twelve pounds to feed them, so the total expenditure was twenty-two pounds, leaving a profit of eight pounds. That was the beginning of the pig business for me and for the next eighteen years the pig fattening remained profitable.

The fair days in Creeslough were almost a thing of the past in the early 1960's. Creeslough fair was always held on the 10th of every month and for a few years after the buying and selling of cattle stopped, people would still go to Creeslough on the 10th. There would sometimes be a tractor and trailer there with pigs for sale and the man selling the cloths would be there. People wanted to hold on to the custom of the fair, as they still liked to go there and do their shopping, meet their neighbours and maybe buy a coat or a pair of trousers from the cloth stall.

It was a wet Friday, I think it was the 10th of April in the year 1961. After my success with the two pigs I thought I might go and see if there were any pigs at the Creeslough fair. When I landed there the first thing I saw at the "corner of the garden", (that was where all the dealing was done), was a man with twelve pigs in a trailer. A woman was trying to buy two pigs from him and he was asking her £12 for the two.

I approached him and asked, "How much do you want for the twelve?" The poor man did not know what to say, as people in those days did not usually buy more than two pigs. Paddy McCarry from Kildarragh was standing looking into the trailer and immediately slapped the man on the back and said," Aye that's the way to talk, what will you take for the twelve?" That was a typical way of dealing in those days where a third man would enter into the deal. If the seller was asking say, seventy pounds and the buyer was offering sixty the third man, or outsider if you like, would suggest to split the difference and after a bit of hand slapping, this sort of dealing might continue until the deal was completed. At that stage they would all make their way to the pub where the seller, after being paid, would "stand" a drink and of course the man who helped with the deal would also get a drink.

I bought the twelve pigs for £60. After that I kept increasing the number of pigs until I was feeding about forty at one time. I was then sending about one hundred and twenty pigs to the bacon factory each year. For the next ten years pigs were a good business to be in. I was making a profit of £5 per pig which was very good money at the time.

In 1961 I bought my first car. It was an Austin A35, which I bought in McElhinney's Garage. The car cost £190.00 along with my motorbike. I thought "That's it now; I have made it, my own car, a good job, what more could I want?"

In August of that year my brother John got married to Dymphna McFadden from Downings. They were married in Dublin and the reception was held in the Shelburne Hotel. I was his best man and I was very nervous on account of it being in Dublin and especially because it was in such a posh hotel.

When I came back after the wedding it took me a while to adjust to being on my own with just my father and mother. John and I were always together as neither of us ever went away to work like a lot of our neighbours. But, it was not very long till something else happened that would take up that space in my life.

One Sunday night I went to a dance in the Creeslough hall, and was very proud of myself with my nice wee Austin. It was the 29th of October 1961 and it was there, that I met Tessie Wilkinson from Faymore. Tessie and I married in August 1965.

Tessie was not unknown to me as I often called into her house and got the tea. We were also in the Legion of Mary together and in Sara McCaffrey's dramatic society (we played husband and wife in a few plays). So, we were not strangers!

Life was fairly busy then. I kept around forty pigs, planted potatoes, corn and hay and milked twelve cows as well as selling insurance. In 1962 I bought my first brand new car, which was an Austin mini. I traded in my Austin 35 in McAuley's garage, Letterkenny and I had to pay £250.00 along with it for the new car. The list price of the mini was five hundred and five pounds and ten shillings.

In 1963 I started making preparations to build a house. I started to clear the site, which was in the garden adjacent to the old family house and there were apple trees growing there. One Saturday my brother Hugh and myself started to clear part of the site with picks and shovels. We started to uproot one of the apple trees and we found it much more of a challenge than we had thought. So, after spending all day digging and cutting roots, all we had to show for our tough day's work was one tree uprooted. It did not take much calculation to discover that eight apple trees would take eight days, not to talk about all the clay that would have to be wheeled with a wheelbarrow, we decided to get a bulldozer.

Bulldozers were not very plentiful but there was one working with the county council about a mile down the road. The next day I went down and asked the man if he would do the job of clearing my site and he said he would be up on Friday evening. Come Friday evening he arrived with his bulldozer and it was the biggest machine that I had ever seen. He just put down the blade and started pushing the soil and the trees and everything else that came in his way, right back to the back of the garden. When he had finished I asked him what he had to get, he looked at his watch and said, "Well, I charge two pounds per hour so by the time I am back to where I was working it will just be two hours." I gave him the four pounds with five shillings of a tip. Considering the time spent by Hugh and myself taking out one tree, it was very good value.

It took almost two years to get the house finished as I was doing most of the work myself. Very few people took out loans or mortgages in those days. I was doing well at the pigs so I went into the bank manager in Dunfanaghy and told him that I was building a house and he advised me he would set up overdraft facilities for me for £500. I paid for everything as I went along so when the house was finished it was all paid for within one year.

With the help and advice of a very good friend of mine, Neil Sheridan from Drimeasson, who was a contractor himself, I put in the foundations and left everything ready for the building. I employed Danny Ward from Drimnacarry to start the block work and he left it ready for the first storey lintels. Then I thought I could continue on my own so I got the help of Timothy Diver from Derryherriff. I did the building and Timothy attended me carrying blocks and mortar. Timothy and I continued until we had it ready for the roof and at that stage we had to employ Packie Langan to put on the roof and do the plastering.

The rest of the work, including the wiring and plumbing, I finished myself. Some years before that, after the factory started, my mother opened a little shop in her own sitting room and as the numbers of workers grew in the factory so the business expanded. She needed more space for the shop so it was incorporated in our new house. The shop continued there until it closed in 1984. The total cost of the three-bedroom house was eleven hundred pounds.

On the 9th August 1965 at 9.30am, in St. Michael The Archangel Church in Cashelmore, Tessie Wilkinson and myself were married. Fr. Deeney married us, with Fr. Godfrey from the Franciscan Friary Ards assisting. The reception was held in McFadden's Hotel, Gortahork. Leo Brennan played the music at the reception and also played the organ at the marriage ceremony.

After the meal the dancing started and continued until about 3.30pm. It was the custom then to go somewhere else for an evening meal, so we all set off for Friel's in Raphoe. We had another meal there and then we started the dancing again. Mind you, the only music we had was Tessies' brother John playing an accordion and my self-doing the singing. I think I must have been the only groom to play the music at his own wedding!

Our honeymoon was spent in Edinburgh and this was also the first time we ever went on a car ferry. Car ferries were not very common then and we did not know what to expect. We stayed in a hotel in Belfast on the night of the wedding and then the following afternoon we went to Donegall pier to board the ferry. When we arrived Tessie was asked to get out and walk on to the ferry while I had to go to the other end of the boat and drive up a ramp, which was very steep, and then stop at the top of the ramp. Three cars were driven up at one time and then we were turned around and had to drive down into the hold of the boat. Some nervous drivers got into terrible trouble.

After getting married I continued selling insurance and fattening pigs. I upgraded the old hen houses by putting in new floors with bottles all lined in under the concrete. The bottles served as a cavity, which kept the floor dry and warm as the heat from the pigs as they lay on the floor built up under them. I could fatten fifty to sixty pigs three times a year; which was good.

In the mid 1950's my father had built a new byre to house six cows which I then extended in the mid 1960's and increased my cows to ten. Every small farmer then was encouraged to send milk to the creamery. There was an agricultural instructor assigned to the area and his name was Sean Geaney. Sean was a big help to farmers as he instructed and encouraged them to increase their cows and improve their small farms. There were grants for farmers who enlarged their stock and improved their land by liming and drainage and any other method that yielded better crops. There was not as much machinery connected with the milk business then. When men with small herds – four to ten cows – started to send milk to the creamery the cows were hand-milked.

I was hand-milking eight cows before I got a milking machine. With the machine the milk was strained into a ten gallon can and cooled with a water cooler that was placed in the can with the water running down the outside of the can. It did the job all right those days, but there is a lot more equipment needed now.

In the summer I was sending about thirty gallons of milk to the creamery every day. So, between the insurance, the pigs and the milk, I did not have much time to spare but we still took time out to have a few days and sometimes a week on holiday.

At that time the area I was covering for the insurance job was increased. It was extended from Kilmacrennan to Kelly's Mills in Letterkenny and from there to the halfway house, now the Silver Tessie, half way between Letterkenny and Ramelton.

As I was working then most of the time around the town of Letterkenny I came into contact more often with Hughie Hone, which was some times a good thing and other times not so good.

One day I had an appointment to meet him at Kilmacrennan at 11am. At the time I was building an extension onto the house and that morning I forgot all about the appointment and was happily working away at a floor I was laying. I was up a ladder in the new extension hammering nails into the floor when I heard Tessie talking to someone. At first I did not recognise the voice but then I heard "What the bucking hell is this man doing?" which was a usual expression of his.

There was nothing for it but face the music. When I came down Tessie was telling him to keep quiet and she would make us tea. After a big bit of giving out and scolding he settled down and took the tea. When the tea was taken he said, "What are you doing anyway?" So I told him I was putting a floor in the new extension. He went up the ladder, took a look at the job and said, "Have you any overalls a man could wear?" I got him the overalls and he worked with me until nine o'clock that night. Of course he was a very good carpenter, and that was the sort of man Hughie was.

Chapter 13 – My Music Career

During the 1960's the idea of the singing pub became very popular. Leo Brennan was one of the first musicians to play in the Donegal pubs. I remember he used to play in Mc Fadden's of Gortahork during the summer and the place would be packed every night.

Dunfanaghy and Portnablagh were becoming busy with holiday makers at that time. The Portnablagh Hotel was a very popular venue and the biggest hotel around. The Sheephaven Hotel in Portnablagh was also popular, especially with the locals. The third hotel in Portnablagh was the Pier Hotel which was the centre spot for entertainment and many big bands played there throughout the year, but mainly in the summer months.

In Dunfanaghy there was the Carrig Rua Hotel and Arnold's Hotel. Tourists were known locally as 'the bathers' which, I suppose was because not many of the locals could swim and seldom bothered to bathe. All the tourists who came from Belfast and Northern Ireland seemed to be able to swim, and they were to be seen every day on the beaches and, as cars were not as common then, they were more to be seen walking around the road between Dunfanaghy and Portnablagh.

In addition to the two hotels, there were four pubs in Dunfanaghy in the 1960's. Jim O'Donnell's pub started music towards the end of the 1960's where Kevin Ward and Arthur Alcorn played seven nights a week to a full house.

In 1971 I retired from New Ireland Assurance and I intended to increase my cow heard and build a pig unit. The main reason I retired, along with wanting to move on from trying to sell insurance, was to get more into farming. I suppose, if I were to tell you the truth, I didn't have a hard enough neck for the job of selling insurance. Anyway, one day at the end of June, I was out in the field working at hay when Tessie came out and told me that Dan Devine from Dunfanaghy wanted to see me.

I went into the house with Dan and he told me that he was thinking of starting music in his pub and wondered if I would sing for him. I couldn't help but think of the story that was told about Dan. In those days, long before singing pubs were ever thought about, it was considered bad practice to allow anyone to sing in a pub. One night there was a big crowd in Dan's, mostly from Horn Head, and someone was making shapes to sing. One of his mates said to Dan, "Would it be any harm if Harry sang a song?" Dan put his two hands down on the counter and said "Man dear, there would be no harm in it at all, but there is just no call for it." I suppose he'd changed his tune, so to speak!

Singing was something I always liked to do but I had not sung much since my days with the band back in the 1950's and 1960's. Anyway, I told Dan I would think about it and let him know. His view was that it was getting to the stage where if you did not have music you would not get the people to come in to the pub.

I gave it some thought and decided that if I was going to do it I would need someone who would sing along with me, not that I was shy, but there were other considerations. Firstly, I wouldn't have enough songs to keep me going for a full night and secondly, I thought it would look better with two people singing. But finding someone who could sing, play an instrument and be willing to sing in a pub, was not going to be easy.

I thought of a young fellow from Ards who was about fifteen at the time, and a very good singer, Ben Mc Fadden. Although Ben was still in his teens he had the advantage of spending a good lot of time around the Franciscan Friary, and he had a bit of training singing in the choir. I realise that singing in a pub would be far removed from hymn singing but at least he knew how to use his voice. I went to see Ben and, after a bit of persuasion and telling him about the money he would make, he said he would give it a trial.

We got together for the next few nights to establish what kind of 'repertoire' we had and what our act might be. I could play in the keys of D and C while Ben could play in D and A which meant that I had to learn to play in the key of A and Ben had to learn the key of C.

We practised for a few nights and felt we were getting on well, but we were afraid we might not have enough songs to last for a whole night's singing. Between us we had about thirty full songs and another ten or so bits and pieces of songs. We knew we would have to sing for about two and a half hours and we estimated that, at the rate of five minutes to the song, including a break, thirty songs would do us for the night. We also hoped there would be some participation by the audience, which would fill up some time.

Neither of us had any previous experience singing in a pub. I had sung in concerts and with the band some years previously but singing in a pub was completely different. In a pub you were expected to be able to keep a sing-song going and get people from the floor to come on stage and perform. We didn't know if we had that ability.

Kevin Ward and Arthur Alcorn had been singing in O' Donnell's pub for a few years and had gained some experience so I met Kevin one day and asked him if he would give me some hints on how to approach a night's singing. Kevin agreed and gave me a few pointers on the best way to get a sing-song going and the best type of songs to sing.

So, all prepared, we started in Dan's Bar in Dunfanaghy towards the end of June, playing just at the weekends. Then, from the beginning of July, we played seven nights a week until the first week of September. Our pay was four pounds per night, two pounds each which doesn't seem very much now, but when you consider that a labourer's pay was only eighteen pounds a week, it was good money for only three hours.

Dan's Bar was a very popular pub with a good mixture of local people and tourists. In those days all the local people who'd left but came back home on holiday came into the town for a nights crack and brought the whole family with them. Many of the local clientele in Dan's Bar were from Horn Head and I would venture to say that it would be difficult to find a better crowd of people for enjoying themselves and having a good night's fun. The Horn Head folk produced some of the best singers and characters you were ever likely to meet.

It would take a whole book to name all the people from there who could entertain either by song, story or recitation. However, when you talk about entertainers from Horn Head, one man has to be mentioned, and that man was 'Harry the Burn'. Harry Alcorn was his name but as most people there had a nickname, he was called 'The Burn'. Harry could sing ballads from all over the country and some from other countries but, you had to know how to handle him. He would not sing early in the night, for two reasons. One was because, as he would say himself, he had not enough 'bird seed' in him. The other reason was he wanted to wait until he had a good audience.

In those years there was a family originally from Horn Head, now living in Glasgow, who came every summer on holiday and their name was Mc Laughlin. They were three brothers – Robert, John and Christy, and another friend of theirs from Glasgow. They played music as a group in Glasgow and would play around Donegal when they came here on holiday. We were very fortunate to have them come into Dan's at least a few nights every week as it made our job a lot easier. They were very good entertainers.

We had no amplification, just two guitars. Dan had a small amp, one microphone and one speaker hung up on the wall. One of us would sing a few songs and then pass the microphone over to the other.

Our first two nights at Dan's were the worst but after that we got to know the people who would come up and sing so that made it a lot easier on us. We soon found that audience participation was what made good entertainment. Our first year there was very enjoyable but we lacked confidence to start with. Gradually we discovered that you did not have to be a top class singer to entertain people – you just need to be natural and let things happen.

In those years I would say that people were much easier to entertain and there was much more fun in the pubs. They did not need a sophisticated show, just good plain singing and music. I still meet people when I'm singing in different places, who talk about the nights we had in Dan's.

We sung for two summers in Dan's pub. At the end of the second year I was playing there one night on my own when I was approached by a man and his wife who were in the audience during the singsong. The man asked me if I ever sang in Letterkenny and I told him I had not ventured that far yet. He said his name was Pat Dunnion and he ran a pub called 'The Hideout' in Letterkenny and he wondered if I would play for him. I told him I would be glad to so he said "Come up and try a night and see how it goes." Thanks to Pat this was really the beginning of my singing career.

I realized now that I needed more than just a guitar to be prepared for playing in other pubs so I went to Joe Deehan in Letterkenny. Joe was the man you had to see in those days if you wanted anything in the amplification line. Now Joe Deehan was a musician himself and a very good man at electronics. He was also a perfectionist and did not have much patience with beginners. That said, I always respected Joe and got on well with him. Joe used to say "You need gear that you can go into any man's town with." I got kitted out with an amp, Goodman's speakers and a microphone.

I played in The Hide Out once a month and gained a lot of experience there. The Hide Out was full of characters that went around the pubs performing in each one they went to. There were also plenty of loyal customers who were there every Friday night and many of them would come up and do their party piece.

Soon after gaining experience in The Hide Out I started singing in pubs all over the northwest of Ireland. During the autumn, winter and spring seasons pubs only had music at weekends but then in the summer months, particularly around the seaside areas, there would be music every night. Music continued like that through out the 1970's and 1980's when bands played most of the music.

I was one of the few one-man shows on the road. At that time lounge bars with dancing areas were popular and groups usually played there. Some of the dance halls were still going and that was where the show bands performed. Towards the end of the 1970's dance halls became less popular and eventually came to an end. This coincided with pubs extending their lounges to facilitate dancing and discos. The big bands moved to play there for a few years but they went into decline too as discos took over from live music. In the early 1980's three and four man groups found it hard to exist and, as a result, a number of them split up into two-man and one-man outfits.

In the singing pubs the old ballads were always very popular, especially with the returned American visitors. Along with the ballads and American country songs, I specialized in songs from the 1950's and 1960's. Songs from Johnny Cash, Buddy Holly, Hank Williams, Jim Reeves, Pat Boon, Michael Holliday, Dean Martin, and of course, Elvis (although I personally was never much of an Elvis fan). Songs like "I Walk the Line" by Johnny Cash, "Oh Boy" by Buddy Holly, "Little old Wine Drinker, Me" from Dean Martin and "Love Letters in The Sand" by Pat Boone; I could go on and on. These songs are still popular today. It's fair to say at that time, the lead singer was the person who was best known. Nobody knew for instance, what the name of the band backing Jim Reeves was; the singer was the main star.

On the dance band circuit in the 1960's and 1970's I suppose Big Tom and the Mainliners was one of the biggest and most popular bands around and they are still going today. There were many other popular show bands in those years too, some of which I have already mentioned.

Social evenings were very popular in the Church of Ireland Hall, Dunfanaghy, in those years. Johnny Gallagher (known as "Johnny Jenny" from Falcarragh), who used to play with the Slieve Foy during the 1950's, sometimes provided the music for these monthly socials, along with Jack Smith. Johnny was a very good accordion player and, after I was invited to sing at one of the socials with them, Johnny, Jack and I soon became a regular band at these dances. The Social's, as they were known, were very enjoyable events where people gathered in around 10.30pm for dancing and refreshments. No alcohol was served, nor was it needed for everyone to have a good time.

Johnny and I often played together at weddings and Irish nights around Falcarragh and Gweedore. For a short period we had a three-piece band with Johnny's son John playing drums. Johnny was also an Insurance agent and worked for Irish Life Insurance Company.

In the summertime, we would play for Mr McElhinney and his guests in the Round Room at Glenveagh Castle. Usually there would be no more than eight or ten special guests and we would play and sing all the old Donegal ballads. On a few occasions we played in the big dining hall when there would be a larger number of guests. In 1983 the castle was handed over to the state and it is now part of a National Park for everyone to enjoy.

Other bands also played at the socials, and one of these was Edwin Moore and his brother Geddy. They also had Jack Smith playing drums and sometimes Hughie Mc Laughlin, better known as Hughie Anton. Occasionally I would play with them at the socials and other functions in the parish. One time we were playing at a fundraising dance, for which Master Cannon printed the posters. The band had just been named sometime before that as The Anvil Ceili Band, which consisted of Edwin and Geddy Moore on accordion, Seamus Lafferty accordion, Eamon Cannon, known as the 'Master', on fiddle and Jack Smith on drums, a position which Richard Druce filled later. When the poster appeared it read "The Anvil Ceili Band" augmented by Seamus Harkin. I'm not sure any of us really knew what "augmented" meant!

In the 1970's a number of groups were going to London and Glasgow and other big cities in England and Scotland to play in the Irish venues and seek their fortune. During 1977 I got in contact with a man who was originally from Kilmacrennan called John Crerand. John was a promoter and acted as a sort of agent for different singers, setting up bookings for them in pubs and clubs in London, Birmingham and Leeds. He set up twelve bookings for me in London in June of that year. The first week was a public holiday because of Queen Elizabeth's silver jubilee and London was crowded with people.

I was supposed to go on the Saturday but, on Thursday night, John rang me and asked me if I could be over on the Friday instead. He told me he had got two more bookings for me on the Friday and Saturday nights, which were very important as the venue was paying £45 (sterling) each night. A fee of £45 sterling at that time was the equivalent of one-and-a-half week's pay. Needless to say, I headed off right away.

So, on the Thursday, with Tessie accompanying me, we set off for Dublin. The plan was that this trip was going to be a working holiday. I had just bought a second hand Fiat car so we got all the gear packed into the car and caught the ferry from Dublin to Liverpool. We had never been to London before so it was a big adventure for us. I had negotiated my way around cities like Dublin, Glasgow, Belfast, and Edinburgh but somehow London seemed a bigger challenge.

We had a night sailing from Dublin so we arrived in Liverpool about 6am on Friday morning. Breakfast was served on the ferry as it docked so we were able to head for the motorway as soon as we landed. The morning was bright and sunny and the heavy traffic had not yet begun so we found it easy to get on the motorway. It was my first time to drive so far on a motorway and it was all very new to me.

After a while motorway driving became a pleasant experience. Every twenty miles or so we passed a service area where refreshments were served. At one of these stations we stopped and freshened up, had something to eat and got petrol before continuing our journey.

We had arranged to meet John at the back of Kings Cross station, beside the taxi rank. As we approached London city, it was a bit scary with the build up of traffic and not knowing where we were going. Tessie was my navigator and, with map in hand, she gave the directions and we soon discovered that our route was reasonably simple as Kings Cross was very well sign posted.

As we sat at Kings Cross station awaiting the arrival of John, we wondered if we would know him when he did arrive. It was now about twelve o'clock midday and there was a lot of activity at Kings Cross. I had told him I would be in a blue Fiat car but he did not tell me what he looked like. John had a brother in Kilmacrennan who I knew well, his name was Charlie, and I wondered if I would recognise him on Charlie. Well, we waited for what seemed a good while watching everyone coming towards us, thinking this could be him.

We had not paid any attention to a man who walked up to the car and said "Seamus Harkin?" "Yes," I replied to which he said "John Crerand. You thought I would look like my brother at home, didn't you?" he said. He was a small man with a long black overcoat, bald on top with long black hair down to his shoulders, nothing like his brother Charlie at all.

John got into the car and he directed me to his house, which was only a few streets away from the station. Upon arriving at his house we met his wife, who was from Kerrykeel. She soon had a meal ready for us and made us feel very welcome.

That night I went to play in my first London pub and, except for one night, I played every night for the next fortnight. John was a chef and worked in a local hospital where he was finished every day at 1pm. This suited his agent's business well as he was free in the evenings and was able to go with me to every pub. John was well known all over London and was a great man to tell a story, a few of which he told about his hometown of Kilmacrennan. He returned home every year to visit his home place and would meet with the local people and get all the latest news.

One story he told was about a man he used to meet who was a musician and who fancied himself and thought he was very good. Now this man used to play in the local hall and jealously guarded this position, so you could imagine his disappointment when another musician replaced him. On one of John's visits he enquired from this man, how the dances were going in the hall. He looked at John and said, "Do you know what I'm going to tell you. The people that are going now know nothing about good music; sure they would dance to a man sharpening a scythe."

I also remember him telling about going home to his native town and calling in to his old local pub. It was in the middle of summer when the pub was full of English visitors. When he entered the pub, Jim, the proprietor, was behind the bar and he shook hands with John and welcomed him home. As he sat on the bar stool drinking his pint Jim said "You must be a good while in London now, John?" "Aye" says John, "Fourteen years, Jim." "And I'd say there's houses there, you weren't in yet," was Jim's reply.

John Crerand was an interesting man with great stories to tell. In describing his career, he told me of the time he went to the Bogs of Allen in County Wicklow to the cutting of the turf when he was a young man. He said "I was no turf cutter, so they sent me to the mess hall to do the tea making and whatever wee bit of cooking was to be done, so that's where I started cooking." After that he joined the RAF and advanced his cooking skills a bit further. While he was with the Air Force, he was trained in making announcements and learned to speak with a very proper English accent. He used this skill to great advantage when he would get up to speak in pubs and clubs but, off the stage, he went back to his native Kilmacrennan accent. Then for many years he worked as a cook for British Rail on the train from London to Glasgow. When he retired from British Rail, he worked as a cook in a hospital beside Kings Cross station, where he worked until his retirement.

Singing in London was a good experience and very enjoyable, it was different from singing at home. Apart from the few Creeslough people I met in pubs, everyone was unknown to me, which meant that I could put on more of a show and not feel self-conscious. I also found that the people listened more to the songs and gave a good response at the end of the song.

I got a very good reaction to my London gigs and was asked to come back in November of that year which I did. November was different as it was more like work because Tessie was not with me and it did not have the same holiday atmosphere, but I still enjoyed it and it was a great confidence booster. I never went back to London to sing after that as there was plenty of music work at home.

The end of the 1970's and early 1980's was a boom time in the pubs around Donegal. In the summer of 1978 I played a gig in the Bagot Inn in Dublin. Jim Mc Gettigan, another Kilmacrennan man, owned it and he booked me as the warm up act for the Ailagh Folk from Inishowen. The Ailagh Folk was a very popular traditional and Irish band at the time lead by Dinny McLaughlin, one of the best fiddle players in the country.

I went to Glasgow that year too when I was invited over to play at a dance in the Plaza Ballroom to raise money for the Creeslough Chapel. Now that was a daunting experience! There were twelve hundred people in the hall with a six-piece band as the main act. Before the dance, the manager of the band asked me if I could sing for two hours, as the main band would only play for two hours. So they started the show and played for an hour and when they were finished, they just announced me and walked off the stage.

I never felt so bad in my life. You can imagine what it was like walking on a big stage all alone, after six band members with all the sound they had, walked off. After plugging in my guitar to one of the many amplifiers and picking a microphone from one of the six available, I said hello to the crowd and started to sing. To me, the whole thing sounded terrible and I never felt so nervous on a stage in my life but when the people started to dance, the old adrenaline started to flow and everything was great for the rest of the night. I played for two hours, after which the main band came back and played the last hour.

On the Sunday night in Glasgow I played in the Claddagh Club which was a very enjoyable night as there was a lot of people I knew and the atmosphere was brilliant, with people from the floor coming up to sing. I was often asked back to Glasgow which I would have loved to do but I never seemed to get the time.

In 1978 I went into Joe Deehan's shop and he said "I have just the machine for you." He produced this very large piece of equipment, like an amplifier with a big speaker built in, which he then opened up and started to play. It was the first electronic one-man-band that ever came into the country. You could sit and play your guitar and sing whilst playing the pedals with your feet to create the accompaniment of drums, piano, organ and bass.

It took me about a month to get the hang of it and to be able to play it well enough to use in public. Joe's stern warning was "Don't take it out to a pub until you can play it without looking at your feet." With this equipment, I could fulfil engagements anywhere so I took bookings for weddings, dances and dinner dances.

Chapter 14 - The Singing Undertaker

In 1978 the music business was doing very well and I was very busy playing in the many pubs and hotels around Donegal. At the start of the year Edmund Boyle, who was the undertaker in the Creeslough area at that time, approached me and asked if I would take over the business.

Eddie Boyle, Edmund's father, had started the undertaking business in Creeslough in the 1930's and he also ran a hackney cab business at the same time. Edmund returned from America in the early 1970's and took over both the hackney cab and undertaking businesses. He then started with the construction business, which did not fit in to well with the undertaking which is when he asked me if I would be interested in taking over the undertaking.

I told him I would think about it and let him know in due course. Tessie and I discussed it and thought we might as well give it a trial. A few days later I contacted Edmund and told him I would take on the business. He had a stock of coffins, which he delivered to me the next day. He said "My father still owns the hearse and you will have to buy it from him," which I did; it was an old Vauxhall.

Now that I had the hearse and the coffins I was ready for business; all I needed was a client. Soon enough, on the 20th of February, I received a phone call to say that Hannah McGinley of Ards had died. Hannah had died in Letterkenny hospital so I had to make the arrangements to take her remains back to Ards. In the mortuary in Letterkenny hospital the mortician at that time was a man called Hugo Doherty. Hugo was a very good mortician and he helped me a lot. Hannah was buried on the 22nd of February, 1978.

It was peculiar that my second funeral was her next-door neighbour, Josie McFadden. Josie was the local postman and was very well known in the area. It was a Saturday morning and he was getting shrubs down in Faugher when he took a heart attack and died in his car by the roadside.

Josie was one of the great characters of the area and many stories were told about him. When he first started delivering post, he was supposed to do it on a bicycle. The rules at that time for the postman were very strict. An inspector would come out and travel around with him to see that he was travelling by bicycle and doing his job properly. Josie delivered the post in all kinds of vehicles. One day he would have a car, the next day maybe a bicycle and he would also use the tractor. Of course Josie would know when the inspector was coming out and would be sure to have his bicycle on that day.

It took some time for me to build up confidence in the undertaking business, and for the people to have confidence in me. Of course laying-out bodies was not unknown to me before I took up undertaking, as I helped many times when somebody in the parish had died. As the years passed and my experience grew I became used to the business and the people became used to me.

The undertaking and singing was a good combination, as it meant that I was mostly free during the day and, even if I had a booking in a pub, I could always get another musician to take my place. For the first few years after starting the undertaking I was still doing some farm work too but then I decided to sell off some of the cattle and only kept young animals.

A lot of interesting stories could be told about wakes and funerals and the customs and traditions surrounding them. Throughout this book I have mentioned a few of them but there is one wake and funeral that for me is very memorable and I think it gives a good idea of a typical wake and burial in the Creeslough/Dunfanaghy area.

It was Christmas Eve. My wife Tessie and I, and the family, went to midnight Mass. It is still called midnight Mass, even though it is held at 9pm. With the crib and the carol singing and the seasonal hymns you could sense the Christmas spirit in the air. The night Mass is a good place to meet all the people who have come home for Christmas. The night being good, people stood around talking and wishing each other a Happy Christmas and welcoming all the people who had come home. It is a time when absent friends are talked about and those who have passed away during the past year are missed.

We arrived home about 10.30pm switching on all the lights and lighting the candle in the window. The presents were all around the Christmas tree and, with the decorations, the log fire burning in the grate and all the family at home, it was now really Christmas. In our house it has always been a custom to have a pot of soup when we return from midnight Mass so this particular year, as usual, we all sat down with our bowl of soup and talked together about everything that happened during the year.

It was about 11.30pm, still too early to open the presents, as we have a rule that presents are not opened until midnight. So we took more soup and wheaten scones until it was time to open the presents. We had great fun looking at all our gifts and were then preparing to go to bed when the phone rang. When the phone rings in our house at that time of night it usually means that someone is dead. As an undertaker I am used to that, but Christmas is a time when I would rather not have to go to work. Of course death doesn't wait, even at Christmas.

The person on the phone said, "This is Doctor O'Hay, I am in McHugh's house in Horn Head. Tommy has died suddenly, can you come over?" Tommy was around seventy but was not considered old as he still worked on the farm and was a very fresh man. He had been to the Christmas Eve Mass at nine o'clock and was not long home when he died.

That was the end of my relaxed Christmas Eve. I got my bag and headed for Horn Head. It was a mild and clear night with the sky glittering with stars as I drove to Horn Head. With the sea washing in on the rocky shore, the natural beauty seemed to add to the solemnity of the night. The Christmas lights were to be seen in all the windows with candles glistening through the window panes. As I drove along, I thought of all the little children unable to sleep with excitement as they thought of Santa coming down the chimney. Little did they know, tucked up in their beds, that as they were thinking of Santa, a soul was called away from this earth.

As I arrived at the house a lot of neighbours had already gathered. I first sympathised with Tommy's wife and his sister and then went to the room where he died. The doctor was still there and said Tommy died of a heart attack. At that point one of the neighbour women came and asked me if I would like some tea before I started to lay him out. In the kitchen the neighbours were gathered getting everything touched up, ready for the wake.

We all had tea and sandwiches and talked about the great character that Tommy was. This is one great thing about the custom of wakes in Donegal – the neighbours come in and organise the wake and the undertaker is just one of the team. At that stage, Fr. Bradley had arrived and went into the room where Tommy was lying on the bed. He anointed the body and then came into the kitchen and joined us for some tea. After a few more stories about Tommy it was time for me to lay him out.

As is the custom, two neighbour men came into the room to help me, they carried in the hot water and any other things needed. Of course all during the 'laying out' stories continued to be told about Tommy. When his body was ready, it was time to get Tommy's best suit out of the wardrobe. The coffin was then brought in and Tommy was laid in his last conveyance.

By this time the house was spick and span and ready for the wake to begin. The house was now full of neighbours and friends all working both inside and outside. The teapot was produced again and one woman said, "You better have another sup before you go." Myself and the other two men who had helped me sat into the table and took more tea and scone bread.

It was about 6 am by the time I left. A lovely Christmas morning, the stars were still bright with not a sign of daybreak. Driving down the steep hill into Dunfanaghy was a lovely sight with the full tide shining like silver. The little town was peaceful and quiet with everyone still asleep. In some windows there were Christmas lights burning. In a few hours the town would awaken and children would jump around with excitement at seeing what Santa had brought. The people would soon learn that Tommy was dead in Horn Head and the news would spread all over the parish. When I got home, everyone was still asleep so, careful not to wake anyone, I went to bed.

Tommy's funeral was on the 27th December. It was a typical Horn Head funeral with all the local customs observed. A neighbour man, Robert McElhinney, took charge of the list of men who were to carry Tommy outside the farm boundaries. With his list in his hand, he went around all the people who were going to be carrying the coffin, telling the first four, "You four carry the coffin from the door to the middle of the lane, the next four, from there to the end of the lane," and so on for about six changes till they reached the march ditch. You might think that this was the job of the undertaker, but that is the great thing about local customs – the people get a chance to do it their way and so keep the custom going.

At this stage I had the hearse backed up to the door and the wreaths were carried out and placed in it. The funeral Mass was in Dunfanaghy at 11am. Tommy's wife and relations went to the room where he was laid out, and said their final farewell before the coffin was closed. Two chairs were placed outside the door and the coffin carried out by two neighbours and placed on the chairs. Being a catholic funeral it was at this point that I said the Our Father and three Hail Mary's and sprinkled holy water.

I often think that this is the time that can be very sad and thought provoking as the last man of his name lies in his coffin on those two chairs. I looked around the farmyard at all the tools, his old tractor and implements and the things he thought very important in his life and even worked with the day before he died. Standing at the byre door was his true friend and helper, his old trusted dog, wondering where his master was.

The first four men lifted the coffin onto their shoulders and headed down the lane. I sat in the hearse surrounded by flowers just rolling along a few yards ahead of the coffin, keeping Robert in the rear-view mirror, as he walked in front of the four men carrying the coffin. Robert's hand went up, which meant it was time for a change of carriers. I stopped for a moment as four new men got in place, and then continued at a snail's pace down the lane. As we turned out on to the road and headed westwards, Muckish Mountain stood out clear and bright against the winter sky. Keeping an eye in the mirror, I could see the crowd stretching back up the lane. Some had not even left the house yet.

We were now ready for another change and again Robert brought in another four fresh men. The only noise to be heard was the purr of the hearse engine and the slow step of feet walking behind. The roar of a cow in the field broke the quietness as we passed. As I looked up the field, at a place where every morning Tommy would have fed them, stood about ten cattle and they were all completely still, staring at the crowd of people going down the road. At this point they started to moo; you would almost think they knew what was happening.

At the gate the carriers were changed again. As I stopped while the change took place, I could see the dog standing just inside the gate, his tail wagging and a look of wonderment on his face. I couldn't help but wonder what he was thinking as he watched all the people going down the road and no sign of Tommy.

The gate looked new. When I say new, I mean about ten years old because that would be looked on as being new for a gate on a farm. During the wake, a neighbour told me about Tommy buying the new gate. He got the gate because he was fed up with the old wooden structure that was there to keep in the cows. Tommy went to the hardware shop in Creeslough and bought two new galvanised gates, one for the field above the house and one for the field below the house.

The day he hung the gates, he had only time to put in the gateposts and did not have time to put on the hinge brackets. He said to his neighbour, "I will do that later when I get time, in the mean time I'll tie them to the posts with rope."

The years passed and Tommy never seemed to get the time to hang the gates properly. Often he opened and closed them and cursed to himself about the fact that he never got around to doing the job right. He always thought there would be another day when he would not be so busy. That day never seemed to come for Tommy.

As we moved on with another four fresh men under the coffin, I could imagine Tommy tending those cattle and making sure they were well fed and watered. In my minds eye, I could see him opening and closing those gates with his faithful dog by his side. Now they all stood still except for the odd switch of their tail. His old dog walked back up the field and, standing up above the cattle, he looked back as if to take a last look at his master before continuing back to the house.

As I looked in the mirror, Robert was getting his last team of men in position. Another twenty metres and we were at the march ditch. Stopping for the last time, I went back to the back of the hearse and opened the door. The four men lowered the coffin down and slid it into the hearse with flowers lined on either side, the door was closed and Tommy was on the last stage of his journey to the church.

Many very valuable lessons and experiences are learned from the undertaking business. Sometimes you can get an insight into people's lives during the time of a wake and funeral. From the time a person dies, through the wake, until the burial you are working very closely with the bereaved wife or husband, the sons and daughters and all the family circle.

Often I am called to a house at 2am or 3am after someone has died. It is a very traumatic time for the family and whether the death is sudden or expected it is still a shock when death comes. After the person has been laid out, the room has to be made ready for the wake. The neighbours gather in and help the family with this work, which is a great custom in the country areas. I often help with this work too and as you move about the house you can almost feel the character of the building and the people who lived in it, especially if it is an old house.

Standing on the landing at the top of the stairs in a house where a person has died it is very easy to imagine their life in that house. Often people were born in the same house they've died in. You can imagine a young boy coming up those stairs with his father and mother before being put to bed. Then later on, as a teenager coming in after a nights dancing or some other entertainment. Then as a young man taking his new bride up those stairs filled with joy and romance. Just looking around at the other bedroom doors one can imagine their family all asleep in their beds as children and the nights they had to rise and attend to one of them who was sick or had a bad dream.

Then, one by one, the children all leave home to make a life of their own. Looking at the newel post at the top of the stairs you could see the wear on it from a lifetime of hands being placed there by the family, and the man himself as he made his way up and down those stairs. It is easy to let your mind imagine, as you stand looking at him laid out in his coffin, the many times he came in and out of that room. The early mornings he had to get up to go to work when he would rather have stayed in bed. The late nights he went to bed tired and weary. Then of course there were the occasions when he and his wife had many happy times and fond memories of a long life, much of it spent in that house.

Now that was all over and he would soon leave this earthly dwelling as his wife sits by his side keeping a last vigil. He would have to make one more trip down the stairs, not on his own this time, but carried by his four sons in his coffin. His wife will now have to spend whatever time she has left in this life on her own. She will have her family calling to see her every week but they all have families of their own so their time will be limited.

In my reminiscence I have been referring to a man. The same story could be told about a woman, a mother. She would be even more important to the family in some ways, than a man. In most cases the mother is the one who makes the home. When the children are small she is the one they go to when they are in trouble and she can ease their hurts and pain with a hug and a kiss. The mother is the one who puts all the little touches to the home, and the one who worries about keeping it clean and having everything neat and tidy when people call. When the family comes home for Christmas or other family gatherings, Mammy is there to see that everyone is well looked after. I think a mother's presence is very much felt in a home. You only have to look around the house and see all the little things that only a woman would think of, little nick-knacks that make a house a home.

I think it is sad when the last of the parents die and the house is closed up; just one more home closed in the countryside. Thankfully, over the years, things have changed in that respect. In the early part of the century and up until a number of years ago one of the family, usually a son, would stay with the parents and get married, bringing their spouse into the family home.

When the father and mother died the house would still be lived in and there would be a continuation of the family in that home. Now sons and daughters are moving out of the family home at an early age to make a life of their own, and not returning to live in their old home. That means when the parents die, that long line of family who passed through that home will be ended. Often the house is sold and all those memories that came down through the many years are gone and are unfelt by the new owners. But, as they say, "That's life."

Music was great therapy for me, especially when dealing with very sad bereavements. When playing music everything else is taken from your mind and you can get away from the everyday things of life. As would happen from time to time you could have four or five people die in the one week. Every day and night during that week I would be going around from one wake house to another. At the end of the week there is nothing better than going to a dance hall or pub to play music for two or three hours.

The summer months in those years were very hectic, every night on the road. I think I still have a diary that shows seventy two nights without a break. There was one Saturday in the early 1980's where I was a sponsor at a christening in the morning, did a funeral in the afternoon and played at a wedding in the evening.

In 1980 I recorded a single. I had a good song written by a local songwriter called Andrew McIntyre. The song was entitled "The Maid of Marble Hill." This song had never been recorded before and was very popular in the pubs around the county.

I put the song on tape and took it over to Donal K O'Boyle in Gweedore. Donal had vast knowledge of the music business as he wrote in numerous papers and magazines on the music scene. He listened to the tape and said he would let me know later what he thought of it. I came home and thought that would be the end of it, because I knew he had hundreds of tapes to listen to.

After a week I got a call from Donal saying he liked the tape, but I would need to improve a bit on the singing with particular attention to diction. Recording myself again and improving the quality of the singing I sent another tape to Donal. This time he said "I think we can book the recording studio." He booked a studio in Belfast called "Outlet Records" under the Homespun Label, owned by Mr Billy McBurney. So, myself and Donal headed for Belfast. That was my first time in a recording studio so it was all a bit strange. Donal introduced me to Billy and a man called Crawford Bell. I had never heard of Crawford before and did not realize he was an accomplished country singer. Crawford was also the producer and sound technician.

The session musicians did the entire accompaniment and soon set up the backing tracks. On the B-side I sang an old song my father used to sing entitled "Skibereen." It took from 11am to 6pm to record the two songs.

Even though I did the recording, I think I was never prepared to do the follow up promotion that was needed to sell a record. Mr McBurney said to me that day in his office when the recording was finished, "You'll have to be prepared to get on the road now and promote your record by doing concerts all over the country."

However, that was one thing I knew I wasn't going to do. Donal had told me the same thing. I was too content at home with my wife and family with plenty of gigs around the local circuit. Travelling the country did not appeal to me as I valued the lifestyle I had very much and didn't want to be away from home. In a few weeks the records arrived and it was very exciting just to see the record and to hear it being played. I was satisfied with the fact that I had made a recording.

At that time, there were not as many local radio stations around. There was one pirate station in Letterkenny, I think it was called Donegal Radio. I went to the station, which was in a little hut on the Glencar Road and was interviewed there about my record. I cannot remember the DJ's name but he played The Maid of Marble Hill and gave it a bit of a boost. It was also played on Foyle Radio and Downtown Belfast. In those days if you were fifty miles outside Dublin you hadn't any hope of being played on national radio. The single sold well and I soon had the thousand sold. As I said before, I did not push the sales; I mostly sold them in the pubs I played in and in a few shops. Never the less it made my name known and, as a result, I got many more bookings.

At the end of the 1970's I played with the Coyle Brothers, Michael and Pat, from the Gortahork area. Michael Coyle was one of the best accordion players in Ireland and his brother Pat was a very good guitar player. I did the singing with them at dances, pubs and weddings. At the beginning of 1980 we started arranging a trip to America. We had big posters printed with our pictures on them for the trip but, as the year moved on we discovered it was not looking too promising, so we gave up that idea.

However, later that year Tessie and myself decided we would go to Philadelphia to visit my sister Mary. I was then put in contact with a man called Jim McGill, and he was involved with Irish music in the Philadelphia area. Jim organised ten bookings for me in Irish pubs around Philadelphia for the first three weeks in September. The venues I was to play in were advertised in the local papers and on the radio. It was a most enjoyable experience to see so many people from the Creeslough/Dunfanaghy area coming out to the different venues. Some of these people had been in Philadelphia for over fifty years and a number of them knew my father and remembered him playing the fiddle at country dances before they went away.

The reception I received was tremendous. The system they had there was very good. When the show started, they stopped serving drink and everyone sat and listened, just like a concert. Then after forty minutes, there was a break and the waiters were on the floor again. During the break I went around talking to people and taking requests. I met a few people who had never been back to Ireland since they went out there in the early 1930's. Since then I have been back on four occasions, but I must say the last time I was playing there, things have changed. I found that there was not the same atmosphere in the pubs. It was more like the pubs here at home, where drink is being served all the time and people do not pay so much attention to the singer.

About the year 1985, I started writing the odd song. Song-writing was something I thought I did not have a talent for. One night as I prepared to go out to sing in some pub or other, I was polishing my shoes when the news came on the TV. The newsreader said that two men were shot in Belfast. With just a slight pause, I continued to polish my shoes. As I drove along on my way to the pub I couldn't help but think on how we had become almost immune to this kind of news. This terrible act of the murder of somebody's son, husband or brother did not seem to alarm me the way it should have done. By the time I got home that night I had one verse of a song composed. Before I went to bed I wrote another verse and, the next day, I finished it. The title of the song was "Free from What?"

The title of the song I suppose came from the idea that we all grew up with the notion of freedom and that our country should be free. The question is, free from what? Now I suppose it is natural for the people of a country to want to have charge of their own affairs and their own elected government to run the country. But the people of a country are the most important and everyone's views must be accommodated. If a person is shot because they do not agree with something, where is the freedom there? I have a belief that there is no such thing as complete freedom. Rights and freedom usually clash. I may have a right to something, but if I get my rights I may be infringing on someone else's freedom and vice-versa. Anyway I suppose that is a debate that could go on and on but I captured my thoughts in my song.

Free From What?
I watched the news again tonight, and two more lives were taken.
Some family's left without their dad and I'm not even shaken.
And that's the thing that worries me, for I'm thought a Christian man,
For those two men who died today are fellows of our land.
And then I get to thinking of those men of days gone by,
We are told that they were brave men and were not afraid to die.
They instilled in us a yearning for our country to be free,
But free from what, that's what I ask, will someone please tell me?
Those gallant men of long ago, they fought with courage strong,
Our children of today are told in history and in song.
But I cannot help but wonder, if those men were here today,
Would they now condone the killing, or seek another way?
For the people of this country, I pray to God each day,
That love will grow in every heart and find a better way.
For love it is the answer, and that was God's command.
What kind of freedom do we seek for the people of our land?
So I say stand up as Christians, and not just to command.
Not bitterness and hatred but love and understand.
For peace must start within the heart, that everyone must see.
We may get rights by war and fights, but never will be free.

Chapter 15 – A Change of Lifestyle

On the 14th of November 1986 something happened to me that changed my lifestyle forever. I awoke about eight thirty on Friday morning; Tessie had just got up to get the children ready for school. I had an appointment to see the doctor that morning, as I had had a slight pain in my chest the week before and wanted to get it checked out. The appointment wasn't until about 12 midday, so Tessie told me to have a lie on and she would soon be back from school.

Just then a very severe pain started to build up in my chest, so I thought I'd better get out of bed and downstairs while Tessie was still there. She got a terrible shock when I arrived down and I told her to ring the doctor. The doctor arrived in about half an hour and he gave me an injection and told me to sit on a more comfortable chair. He probably knew that I was having a heart attack as I had already thought that myself.

Soon the ambulance arrived and I was taken to Letterkenny hospital. Tessie had to travel with me in the ambulance and that journey seemed to take forever. Paddy Curran from Letterkenny was on the ambulance and he gave me great encouragement as we went along. Paddy told me that he had a heart attack himself and not to worry, and that I would be all right.

When we arrived at the hospital I was wheeled in on a trolley and taken to the coronary care unit and was all wired up to the heart monitor. A young doctor then questioned me all about my lifestyle, asking questions about smoking, what I did for a living and if I had any relatives who'd died from a heart attack. During all this time Tessie was in the waiting room not knowing what was happening and it must have been a terribly anxious time for her.

After questioning me the young doctor then went to see Tessie in the waiting room and told her that I had had a heart attack and that it would be 48 hours before they would know if I was going to be all right or not. The nurses and doctors couldn't have been more helpful and they were very reassuring at all times. The main reason for the heart attack would seem to have been smoking, coupled with the lifestyle that I lead, playing music in smoke filled bars with a lot of very late nights.

During that first night after the heart attack I lay awake a good lot and my mind started running away with me. I began to think if I would die what would happen, who would do the undertaking? My experience as an undertaker was a good reason for these thoughts I am sure, as I was often called out to someone who had taken a heart attack and died there on the spot. I was sure John Ferry from Falcarragh would do the job as he and I always worked together, I could hear my mother saying "He should be buried in that big oak coffin that he fixed up himself." Then my natural instinct to fight for survival took over and I soon dismissed those thoughts. It seems funny to think back on this now but it wasn't very funny at the time.

Well, thank God, that night passed and all those kinds of thoughts passed as well. After a few days I moved up to the upper end of coronary care, which meant that I was improving. When I moved up there I got a great surprise, as the first man I saw was Johnny Gallagher from Falcarragh. Johnny and I sold insurance at the same time, he sold for Irish Life and I sold for New Ireland. We also played music together and now we were having a heart attack together. We had great crack for a few days and then we were sent to Medical One where we spent the rest of the week.

It was a terrible time for Tessie, as she couldn't move very far from the hospital because she never knew when she would get the call. But she was able to come and collect me the following Saturday and it was great to get back home again. That first night at home was very worrying as I felt on my own without any backup and, of course, I was still very weak.

When I look back now at that first step on the long road to recovery I just cannot believe some of the things I did. It is as if it was someone else, another person who went through this. My first thoughts and attitude was that I was finished with any kind of normal life but thankfully that notion did not last very long. Soon I was getting back to normal living and doing the things I liked to do, especially the music and the odd light job.

The spring following my heart attack, Tessie and I would go walking through Ards Forest Park every day as part of my exercise. I started to pick young beech plants that grew from seed along the roadside and soon I became obsessed with this practice and got Tessie to help pull the seedlings. I would take them home and prepare a ridge in the garden and line them in.

This went on all spring, gathering beech trees and any other young natural plants I could find. I had a plot in the garden with one thousand beach and about five hundred other varieties. I then started to erect a polythene tunnel and again I had Tessie out helping me to put the polythene on the frame. At the time I did not think very much about why I was doing this, it just came naturally. Looking back on that period now, we often laugh at some of the things I did. I think it had something to do with promoting life, as anything that there was life in, I wanted to nurture and propagate.

Over the next few years I continued to write songs. Gradually, after the heart attack, I got back to the singing but never took on the same amount of bookings as I did previously. I selected the venues better and only played in the ones I liked. Playing with the Anvil Ceili Band was very enjoyable, there was not the same pressure I would have had when playing on my own.

In 1992 I did a twelve song album entitled 'Quality of Life', 6 of these songs were my own compositions. I recorded it at Percy Robinson's studio in Letterkenny, which was much more convenient then having to go to Belfast. It took a week in the studio to record the album.

I had a big launch of the album in the Corncutter's Rest in Creeslough and the girl from Donegal herself, Bridie Gallagher, did the honours while two of my good musician friends, Brian McLaughlin and Hugh McLean, provided the backing music for the night. I was pleased Bridie could do it because she is a neighbour and was always very supportive of me and gave me good advice. At that time CD's were very expensive so I just did it on tape and got a few promotional CD's done.

The album sold very well but, like the single I released a few years earlier, I did not put enough effort into its sale. I always have good enthusiasm with the preparing and recording of an album but when it is all done, I seem to fall down on the promotion. It was an ambition of mine to record an album with some of my own songs, which I had now achieved, and that was satisfaction enough for me.

At this stage Highland Radio was up and running and was a great help with the promotion. They gave the album good airplay and I was interviewed a few times on the station. I have to thank one presenter in particular who made my name known all over the north west of Ireland. Sadly, he is no longer with us. His name was Brendan Maxwell.

Brendan and I met for the first time at a wake. As is usual at wakes in Donegal stories are told, so we got into the story telling and Brendan said "I'll have to get you on Highland some night for a crack." At that time Maxwell had a programme on Thursday nights from 11pm to 1am and on these programmes he usually had a singer or storyteller or some other kind of character. I was on with him shortly after our first meeting for one of those sessions and as he would say himself, "We had some crack!" Brendan loved the fact that I was a singer/songwriter and an undertaker as well.

After that we became good friends and he called me the 'singing undertaker.'

Then, one Halloween night, he came to our house and did a programme from the sitting room. I had local singers, storytellers and musicians gathered, much as they would have been years ago, for a nights 'raking.' Brendan had a gift for bringing the best out of everyone yet never had anything prepared, it all happened naturally. He delighted in chaos and could turn it to his advantage.

Over the years we had a number of such nights from our house. These nights were very popular and the people around the area were always asking when we were having another session. Two of the characters who were there on such nights were James Coll and Eddie McClafferty, both now deceased. Eddie published a book of his poems just before he died and from that book he was known as the 'Creeslough Poet.' James Coll could always be relied on for a good story or a recitation.

Mick McGarvey was another of the crew who was always very popular with the listeners and, of course, everything he told was the truth! Ben McFadden, who started off singing with me, would drop in and sing a few songs. Charlie McConnell would recite and John McClafferty would sing. Edwin Moore and Jim Doherty would play some ceili music while Danny McCarry from Kildarragh, who was one of the best fiddle players in the county, was always a popular performer. Danny, sadly, has now gone to his eternal reward.

My brother John was there on one such occasion and he did one or two of his many recitations. Many others would drop in on the night, including Sarah McCaffrey who would have an interesting story to tell, and Dermott MacIntyre who would entertain the listeners with local history. Tessie would have other neighbour women on the night to help with the 'poundies' which were always a traditional meal on Halloween night.

Poundies, of course, are mashed potatoes. On the first of these nights, when the poundies were served, I explained to Brendan and the listeners what the secret of making good poundies was – they had to be free from "juke the beetles" which are little lumps in the poundies.

In the old days, potatoes were mashed with a wooden instrument called a beetle. The beetle had a round end on it and, as it went down through the potatoes little bits of potato would "duck" from under the beetle, hence the name "juke the beetle." As I went on to explain, the word poundies was used to describe someone who was not so intelligent, saying, "He's as thick as poundies." Now a woman, who lived not too far from where I live, called her man "Auld juke the beetle." That meant he was even thicker than poundies!

Halloween was always an important date on the calendar. The original meaning of the word Halloween is "All Hallows Eve", the eve of "All Saints Day." A lot of ghost and witch stories were associated with this time of the year because, I suppose, the day after All Saints Day, the 2nd of November, celebrated by the Catholic Church, was the feast of All Souls. This is a special day of prayer for the souls in purgatory and a lot of superstition and stories are connected with this feast. It was thought that the souls in purgatory would all rise from the dead on that night and come back to their homes.

Some of the old people took this very seriously and would even leave chairs around the fireside on that night and a fire would be left burning. A lot of holy water would be sprinkled around the house, and especially on the doorstep, as it was believed that other spirits like witches would be on the prowl. The holy water would be welcoming to the holy souls but would repel the witches and any other unwelcome spirits.

I always had a keen interest in local characters. When I was a boy growing up, there were a few characters in every townland. Some of them told stories, others sung songs and played music, while others wrote songs and recitations. Two names in the parish of Doe were well known, Andrew MacIntyre and Neil McBride. Andrew wrote many songs, the best known of which were "Deep Sheephaven Bay" and "The Maid of Marble Hill." Andrew became the County Liberian in the library in Lifford and lived there until his death.

Neil wrote many songs and recitations and had a book of his songs published in 1905 entitled "Heather Blossoms". The best known of his songs is "Noreen Bawn." That song has been recorded by many artists and is still popular today, as is the "Hills of Donegal," another much requested song.

There were many other songwriters in the parish who wrote some good songs but never got any recognition and I felt compelled to do something about it. I gathered as much material about all the poets and characters as I could find and compiled it in a book, which I called "Poets and People of Doe," which was published in 1996.

I enjoyed writing the book as I got to know much more about the people and the type of lives they led. This book gave young people from the area an opportunity to know something about these talented people and to see the songs they wrote. I include a recitation entitled "Thon Time," which tells the story of a typical night's raking where neighbours gathered in to our house on a winter night and sat around the turf fire entertaining each other with their stories and songs.

THON TIME

Have you ever sat on a winter's night, with the turf fire burning bright?
And hear the latch a lifting, then someone says "Good night."
"Come on in, John, you're welcome, we'll make the circle wide,
'Tis cold the wind that's blowing, but it's nice and warm inside."
"Come up and pull a chair up, you must be frozen stiff.
I think the snow's not far away, tomorrow could be rough.
Here, fill your pipe and light it, and give your shins a heat;
Get that dog down from the fire, so as John can warm his feet."
"Don't close that door a minute, someone else is coming in,
Oh 'tis yourself, Dan that's in it, be God that wind is thin.
It's a terrible night for some poor man that has to live alone,
You'd be frozen in the bed, without a woman of your own."
Then seated 'round the fire, the stories would begin,
It was like a competition to see which of them would win.
They would talk about the weather and what happened at the fair.
Then John would tell about the day that Mickey yoked the mare.
To listen to their stories, it would scare you half to death,
About the man who fainted when he felt the devil's breath.
And the ghosts they saw on lonely roads when going out to rake,
Or the man that heard the banshee when coming from a wake.
With imagination flowing they could entertain the town,
Then Hughie would tell about the time he worked in the County Down.
And Dan would sing a wee song about the man up from Terlin,
Or about the men in Brocas and what they did way back "thon time."
The kitchen table would then be set and a pot of tea was made,
"Sit over there and take a sup, Dan sit up at the head."
There'd be plenty of homemade butter, and raisin bread to fill the plate,
And maybe a cake of "hard oaten" would sit before the grate.
When the tea and all was over with the fiddle in his han',
Hughie would play the reels and jigs and sing the Candy Man.
Then Dan would sing the story of the work on Muckish san',
And how the old boys "thon time' would smoke from han' to han'.
Then John would say "it's getting late, we better say good night.
I think the wind has settled, and the moon is shining bright.
The nights are at their longest, there is no day in it now,
It will be another month or two, before a man could start to plough."
Those days of long ago have passed, and the men they have all gone,
But the memory of their happy ways in my mind they linger on.
I like to tell the stories; it's the reason for this rhyme,
Of the life they led and the things they said, my memory of "thon time."

Over the years I kept on writing songs and poems. In 1998 I compiled and published another book entitled "As I See It," which contained a collection of all the songs and poems I had written and some of them I'd recorded. As well as songs and poems, I wrote little notes and explanations of why I had written the poems in the first place. The reason I called the book "As I See It" was because different people have their own way of looking at things and I was just giving my way.

In 1999 I recorded an album entitled "At Home on my Donegal Shore." It was a 16-track album, 11 tracks of which I wrote myself. I wrote the title track, "At Home on my Donegal shore" because most of the songs that were written in Ireland were about emigration and those who went way. I thought it was time that a song was written about someone who did not go away and yet did very well at home.

The usual story that was contained in the emigration songs was of a man who left Ireland and the girl next door and went off to seek his fortune only to return many years later to find that she was married or dead and the house he left with the roses all round the door was now tumbled down and deserted. Well, this man stayed at home and married the girl next door and both lived very happily ever after.

Throughout my music career I have always played on a regular basis with the Anvil Ceili Band. The members of the band for the last 25 years have been Edwin Moore from Dunfanaghy on the accordion, Tim Doherty from Kilmacrennan on the fiddle, Richard Druce from Cashel on drums and myself singing and playing guitar on special occasions.

Over the years other people who played with the band included Seamus Lafferty from Faugher, and Jim Curran, also from Faugher. Jim gave up playing the music, in public anyway, and is now working with Donegal County Council. Seamus, along with Ben McFadden from Ards and Patrick Dorrian from Fanad, formed a band and played around the county for a few years. During the years after I had the heart attack I often asked Seamus to accompany me to some venues that might need accordion music and he was also very useful to help me set up the equipment. Seamus was a very good accordion player and was very popular around the pubs of Donegal.

Once I got a very bright flowery shirt which I thought would be nice to wear playing in pubs but, owing to my condition at the time, I felt the cold quite a bit so I also wore a thermal vest which would show around my neck. One weekend Seamus and I were playing mostly in Gweedore, and the weather had improved and the sun was shining. I called to pick up Seamus and, as he got into the van, he took one look at me with my flowery shirt and my thermal vest showing and said, "The sun is splitting the rocks and you still have that thing showing around your neck, either take off the flowery shirt or the thermal vest because the two don't go together." He is now in America and I suppose he hasn't got the time to play music. Seamus was also of great assistance to me in the publishing of two of my previous books and he has written a few words for the Foreward of this book as well.

The trouble with telling stories is that usually you can only tell a particular story once. However, one of these stories became very popular and I found myself been asked to tell it on numerous occasions. I would begin by telling the audience about all the famous people around Donegal, people like Bridie Gallagher, Clannad, Enya, Daniel O'Donnell and others. I told them that in the townland of Knocknafaugher the great-grand-father of Walt Disney was born.

Back in the early 1800's the farmers around the area grew a big crop of lint. The lint was pulled and steeped in a dam for a week and then it was spread out on the field until it dried. It was then gathered up and sent to a scutch mill. One of these mills was in Knocknafaugher and a man came from Ramelton to run the mill, his name was Willie Grey. The people from Ramelton had a different dialect to the people in Knocknafaugher and they added "ney" to a lot of words like "didney," "couldney" and "wouldney."

At the time, turf was the main source of fuel for the fire and everyone went to the bog to cut it. Donkeys were in big demand for taking turf out of the bog and it was a common thing for people to get the loan of a donkey for this job. Now, donkeys have a habit of lying down in the mud or the dust and rolling in it and this was known as 'waltering'. If a donkey waltered with the creels on him he would break them and it would take hours to get them fixed so, as you can see, it was important to have a donkey that did not walter.

Willey Grey had a donkey and when anyone would ask him for the loan of the donkey he would say "You can have him surely and he disney walter." Of course it was not long until Willie was given the nickname Disney Walter.

Now, at that time it was common for the police to go around the countryside to take the tillage or the census. The police never heard any name on Willie other than Disney Walter so they put him down as that name and he was officially known from then on as Disney Walter. Some time later he had a son and called him Charlie. When Charlie was 20 years old, like many others, he went to America. He got married and had a son who he called Disney, for his father.

When Disney went to school he was very good at art and after a few years he became known for his cartoon drawings. A talent scout from a newspaper picked him up and offered him a job doing a cartoon strip for the paper. After only a short time he was much sought after and was becoming famous. At that point his manager suggested that, like other famous people, he might be better changing his name. Disney asked him what he would suggest and his manager said "We will just change it around and call you Walter Disney." So there you have it, straight from the horse's mouth!

Chapter 16 – Butter Making and Goslings

Many times I have been asked to tell stories and talk about local history and about local characters. One such time was at the Workhouse in Dunfanaghy where people would gather in to listen to someone like me talk on some subject of interest.

One time I was there to talk on local customs. I remember it was in the afternoon and the sun was shining through one of the windows and spilling a ray of sunshine across the old flag floor. As I got up to speak I looked at the sunshine lighting up the flags and it immediately reminded me of the day of the churning in the old kitchen at home when I was a boy. So instead of talking about local customs, which was what I was supposed to talk about, I began to talk about churning and making butter.

Everyone made their own homemade butter when I was young and the preparation for it was very interesting. For two weeks before the churning, the cream was gathered in white enamel dishes and each night the milk was strained into them. The strainer was a simple thing that the tinkers used to make and sell to the farmhouses. It was a funnel shaped structure made from tin with muslin cloth tied over the bottom of it.

As the milk sat in the dishes the cream came to the top and it was then skimmed off into a big crockery jar which was an art in itself. First a spoon was run around the inside edge of the dish to separate the cream from the side of the dish, and then the dish was lifted up and, with a slight blow, the cream all ran off the top of the milk into to the crockery jar. Now, as the cream was going in, some of the milk also went into the jar. This was important because when the churning was done there was then enough milk left for the buttermilk. In modern day churning the butter is made from pure cream so there is nothing left for the buttermilk. Buttermilk was a very refreshing drink. On a hot summer day after coming in from the fields, there was nothing as nice as a drink of buttermilk.

Next the churn had to be prepared. After the churn had been washed in boiling water, it was left out on the hedge to dry and to air, if the day was dry and the sun shining. It was then taken to the kitchen and the milk poured from the crock into it. It was left sitting close by the fire until the milk came to room temperature. The churn we had was what was known as a dash turn. It had a shaft standing up in the middle with a round wooden disk at the bottom, which was used to agitate the milk. The churn was then taken to a flat flag in the middle of floor and the churning would begin.

Now, at this stage, if any neighbour came into the house they would usually say, "God bless the work," and if they did not say that, some people might not be pleased. In those days some people believed if they did not say "God bless the work," that might mean they held some sort of grudge against them and the churning might not turn out the best.

It was a belief held by some people that there were those who could "blink" something. Now to blink something meant that they put a curse on it and if they put a course on the churning, there would be no butter. However, there were all kinds of remedies for this. Some people would put burned coals under the churn and others would put pins, which were believed to keep away the evil spirits. Thankfully not too many people believed in this sort of thing.

If conditions were right and if the milk was at the right temperature, then the little beads of butter should start to show in about 15 or 20 minutes. At that point the movement of the staff up and down would be slowed and the butter would form in one big mass. The butter was then lifted out from the milk and placed in a wooden bowl, which would have been washed in boiling water and completely sterilised.

Fresh water, which would have been taken from the spring well earlier, was poured over the butter until all traces of the milk disappeared. During this process the butter would be cut down the middle with a knife and if there was any whiteness in the water that ran from the centre of the butter it would be washed again until all the water ran clear.

While the washing was being done, salt was added to the water and it was mixed well with the butter pats. The next job was known as "hairing" the butter, I am sure it meant de-hairing. To do this, a knife was moved through the butter and if there were any hairs in it they would stick to the knife and therefore be removed. Before the butter was salted a small amount of the butter was taken and kept in a container. This was used later for greasing the axles on the cart and, in the old thatched houses, it was kept behind the purling in the roof. The butter was taken before salting to keep it from rusting the axles on the cart.

When the washing, salting and the de-hairing was completed, the butter was then made into small shapes with the butter pats. There were some nice wooden shapes with prints of fruit and nuts on them and they were stamped on top of the butter. In the summertime, and when the weather was warm, the butter would sometimes be placed in a bucket of cold water and kept there until it would became nice and firm. Of course, there were no fridges in the houses in those days so it was not easy to keep the butter in good shape.

In all farmhouses there was always a dog around the house and, during the churning, he could be very useful for licking up the splashes of milk from the old flag floor that would have sparked out of the churn. When the churning was finished and the butter all made up, the kitchen floor was washed and any splashes of milk that the dog might have missed, would be wiped away. The buttermilk that was left in the churn was placed in a cool spot and used as a refreshing drink until the next churning.

My father told many stories, some true and some not so true. One particular story he told I think was about 75% true. It was about a "clucking" (pronounced "clocking" by local people) hen, that was set on four goose eggs.

When a hen is said to be 'clucking' she would have laid a number of eggs and was preparing to sit on them to hatch them. It is a natural thing for a hen to cluck as she gets a yearning for motherhood. It was a common practice to take a hen that was clucking and set her on a few goose or duck eggs.

Now this one particular hen was set in a big black pot that would have been used for boiling potatoes. Before the hen took up residence there, the dog used it as his bed. The dog had to be kept out of the barn where the hen was sitting on the eggs but every chance he got he was trying to oust the hen off her eggs.

After two weeks the poor hen got fed up fighting with the dog and she abandoned her duties. After that the dog got back his old bed and lay on the eggs and, of course, the heat of his body finished the incubation of the goslings. When the goslings emerged from the eggs they thought the dog was their mother and followed him around. At that time there were plenty of birds and fowl feeding around the farmyard so the goslings had no problem getting plenty to eat.

Now it soon became known that the dog was a very good mother, much better then a hen as he could go into the river with the goslings, whereas the hen could not. As the months passed and the young goslings grew, they and the dog could be found roaming the farm with the dog scraping for seeds and worms for his busy followers. In the morning and the evening when the dog would have to help with putting out and taking home the cows, the goslings would follow as well.

As the young geese grew, three of them drifted away on their own and took up their place with other fowl on the farm. The other one stayed with the dog and the two of them became real pals. Every evening when the dog went out to the fields to take in the cows for milking the young goose would follow. It soon became noticeable that the goose had quite a knack for turning the cows, which were more afraid of the goose than the dog.

This procedure carried on as normal and it was usual for the goose to take in the cows when the dog was not about. It was said that my grandfather Johnny preferred the goose when taking in the cows.

At that time my father bought ten sheep from a neighbour and put them to the hill. We did not have much hill land and the sheep were always breaking down to the fields. Our dog was not a sheep dog and was not able to handle the sheep.

My father then had a plan. He would try the goose with the sheep to see if he would have more success than with the dog and sure enough from the very first time, the goose showed good signs of being able to handle the sheep. After a few months the goose could gather them up or take them from the fields to the hill – she was a natural. The goose was much better than any dog because she did not have to run around the sheep, she could fly over them and land in front of them. When she was turning them in a gap she could flap her wings and hiss at them which no dog could do. That goose went down in history as being the only goose ever known – in these parts at least – to be able to round up cows and sheep.

Chapter 17 - The Millennium

The year 2000 was being talked about for almost 20 years before it happened but, obviously, it was not until 1990 that it really took off and, being big news, the media found lots of stories in the situation. Every area wanted to do something special to mark the occasion. In Dublin they erected a large spike on the old site of Nelson's pillar. In other places they named buildings and others structures to mark the millennium.

In the Creeslough area a few of us had the idea of putting something on Muckish Mountain to commemorate the millennium. While not the highest; Muckish is the most prominent mountain in the northwest of Donegal. For this reason, it was the obvious choice when it came to erecting something. Gerald Duffy of Carnamaddy and myself had a talk about it and we felt that a cross would be the most fitting. Of course, it was not the first time a cross was put on Muckish.

The year 1950 was a holy year all over the Christian world. At that time sand was being quarried on Muckish and was shipped from Ards pier for the manufacture of a specific type of glass. The men who were working there, in their spare time, put together a cross made from railway sleepers and erected it on the east facing summit. It was not blessed in that year as I think the weather was not suitable. The official blessing was on the 15th of August 1951 by Fathers David and Ephrem from Ards Friary.

A large number of people climbed to the summit on that day and were captured in photograph by a Derry Journal reporter. You can see me in the lower right hand corner, a little fair-haired fellow of 16 years of age. Two of my mates are beside me, Paddy Kenny whose mother was Rose Ward from Knocknafaugher and John Harkin from Kildarragh. His mother was known as Bella Doohan, which was her maiden name.

The timber of the old cross had deteriorated over the years and it had almost disappeared completely. Then another, smaller steel cross was erected by Charlie McKinley from Purt, Dunfanaghy, along with a few other people but I do not know what year that was.

Once we had the idea of erecting a cross we called a meeting, which was spent talking about what should be done. A committee was formed and it was decided to hold a weekly meeting from there on. To list everyone involved would be too long a list and the danger of leaving someone out would be great so I will just give the names of the officer board. I was the Chairman, the Secretary was Charlie

Gallagher, the Treasurers were Gerald Duffy and Charlie Doherty and the PR was handled by Brian Ferry.

The committee consisted of at least twenty very enthusiastic people. It was decided to get a galvanised steel cross made which was 20 feet in height and weighed half a ton and, of course, the next problem was how it would be taken up to the summit.

There was an idea of winching it up to the top so a big frame with lorry wheels on it was made and the cross was strapped to it, but after an attempt on a very foggy Sunday morning it was decided to abandon that idea. Investigations were made about the possibility of getting one of the large machines that are used to take trees out of the forest to carry the cross to its destination. In all my time involved in organisations, let it be parish work or others, I do not think I have ever seen a more enthusiastic group. If it had come to the crunch they would have carried it up by hand. We then got the idea of a helicopter airlifting it and flying it to its base on the top of Muckish.

Charlie Gallagher was our man here as he had connections, through the FCA, to the Air Corps. Charlie was successful in getting a helicopter to fly up some of the material, which would be needed for the foundation of the cross and material such as sand, cement and water, along with some tools.

It is not every day you can fly a helicopter to Muckish so we had to wait until we got a good day. Again our team was at the ready to help with this operation. Then one day the clouds lifted off Muckish and the sun came out so it was all systems go. It was exciting to see a helicopter arrive to begin the task. It landed in Willy Wilkins' field in Magharoarty as they needed a large field with no wires crossing it.

Our workers took the sand, cement, water and other things that might be needed to Wilkins' field. The helicopter could only take eight hundredweight each time so the crew had to make about six flights. On each flight one of the workers went to the summit and carried the material to the spot where the cross was to be erected. I went up on one of the flights and it was a memorable experience. Coming down was exhilarating as the helicopter flew out over the edge of the mountain and seemed to drop like a bird on the wing. The working team were not as lucky as I was as they had to come down the mountain on foot.

With that part of the job done it was back to the planning of the big airlift, lifting the cross itself. The Air Corps said the cross was too heavy as it was too much swinging weight and would be very dangerous. Charlie again brought his negotiations skills to bear and got them to agree to try it.

On the 22nd of August 2000 it was a beautiful sunny day with hardly a cloud in the sky. The planned spot for the lift to take place was in John Curran's field in Carnamaddy. It was an ideal place as it was clear, without wires crossing it, and was in close proximity to Muckish. The cross had been taken there the evening before and laid out in the field with white markings around it.

At about 10 o'clock on that morning, people began to gather as the news spread that the helicopter was coming to airlift the cross. People were taking up vantage points along the road and a large crowd had assembled in the field. Then, all of a sudden, a cheer went up as a helicopter made its appearance, coming in over Cruckatee and making its way to the top of Muckish to view the site. Then, to our complete amazement, a second helicopter appeared on the horizon. Soon the two machines had landed in Curran's field. From early morning a large team of men from the Creeslough/Dunfanaghy area had assembled on the summit to prepare for the arrival of the cross and an equally large number of workers had assembled in the field.

The six crew-members, led by Captain Verling, outlined the procedure for the lifting of the cross. One helicopter would do the lifting and the second one would observe the procedure and be there as a backup. Containers of ready mixed concrete, which were brought from Muckish Sand and Gravel by Brian McGinley, were taken up first. Then it was time to hoist the cross itself. I will never forget the site of that silver coloured cross as it swung like a pendulum beneath the helicopter, the sun shining on it like some kind of jewel. In just a few minutes it got smaller and smaller as it ascended towards the summit and the crowd waiting there to receive it.

With the job complete the two helicopters descended back to Curran's field where the women, and the girls and boys, had refreshments of all kinds ready for the crew and all the willing workers. The atmosphere was great as everyone sat around on the grass enjoying a well-deserved meal after such an eventful day. As I sat there and watched the large crowd of helpers along with the six crewmen enjoying the refreshments my mind drifted back to the harvest field of many years ago when it was a common occurrence to see the workers all sit around on sheaves of corn enjoying their meal on a autumn evening. The difference was that two helicopters replaced the two horses and the reaper. It is nice to see that these old customs still surface now and again.

As the evening sun began to sink in the west a little cloud descended on Muckish, just around the area where the cross was now standing, as if to sanction its arrival. Then we all bid a fond farewell, and a safe flight home to the crewmen, and watched them and their machines as they slowly faded from sight over the horizon.

The next and final phase of the project was the blessing and it was decided that the blessing would take place on the 27th of August, 2000. However, on that Sunday, while everything was ready, bad weather came down and we felt it wasn't safe to climb the mountain. We then decided to have the blessing on the 3rd of September and all the clergymen from the different religions were invited to come along.

That day turned out to be the most beautiful day of the whole year. The time was set for people to be up at the cross at 3pm. Many people started gathering about 10 o'clock and from then until three o'clock there was a steady stream of people making their way up from all sides of Muckish. It was so mild and warm that even on the summit it was comfortable to walk around in short sleeves. Midges were to be seen, and felt, up beside the cross.

Along with the people gathered around the cross was Archdeacon Scott Hart and Fr. Patrick McGarvey who did the blessing. We concluded the lovely service by singing The Old Rugged Cross and other hymns. A crowd of approximately eight hundred people climbed the mountain on that day.

Chapter 18 – Writing and other projects

About ten years ago, a very good friend of mine, Neilly McCarry from Kildarragh, and myself were doing some job or other around the farm. We were talking about old times, as we often did, when Neilly started to talk about all the old houses in the parish that had closed and were now derelict. We both agreed that they should be recorded in some way before they disappeared completely and young people would never know that they existed. So, we set out one day with camera in hand, and began to photograph all the old houses where people had built new houses and left the old one derelict, or where people had died out. Neilly's idea was that at least the younger generations would have a chance to see the type of houses their forefathers lived in.

Then about five years ago, a man who has a holiday house in the area, in a place called Roshin, called with me and said he had heard from Neilly that I had some pictures of old cottages and he asked if I would be interested in being a co-author in a book on the old Irish Cottages. This man's name was Clive Symmons and he had a very keen interest in the old Donegal cottages. He also had a good number of pictures himself. Clive had bought one of these old single-story farm cottages many years ago and had restored it to its former glory.

We worked together on this book – I provided the local knowledge and introduced Clive to some of the local people who still lived in these old houses and others who had moved out and built new houses. Clive did most of the research and provided most of the pictures. This book was launched on the 27th of November, 2004 and the title of the book is "The Disappearing Irish Cottage."

Of all the things that happened through out my life there are a few things and occasions that I treasure more than any other (apart from, of course, family events). I am not listing these in any order of importance but they are projects I was pleased to be associated with.

As well as keeping Faugher National School open, another project that I am happy to have been part of was the organising and setting up of the Community Day Centre and St Michael's Housing for the Elderly in Creeslough. This again is a great success and please God will be with us on into the future.

The third highlight was the part I was privileged to play in the community effort of the planning and erection of the Millennium Cross on Muckish Mountain, which I've already talked about.

The one thing in all these projects is the fact that they were all community efforts and were carried out by people who were motivated by a desire to enhance their community, and not for any personal gain. To be part of that spirit of positive action and commitment towards the betterment of the community is very rewarding.

Chapter 19 - Over the Hill

The customs and traditions of old are still very much alive in rural areas. People still help their neighbour, maybe not in the same way they did years ago, but as work practices have changed so have the ways of helping. Young men in the country who are building new houses often help each other in the preparation of the site and other work as the house progresses.

Another custom that survives is that of visiting your neighbour. This might not be on a regular basis but they are there when they are needed. I am glad to say a number of houses still have what used be known as rakers. The house of my next door neighbour, Jack McGarvey, has been a raking house as long as I can remember. A number of us would gather on a Tuesday or Thursday night and we would have a great night's crack and many things would be discussed. Some people referred to it as "Brussels" because there were as many things discussed in it as in Brussels, while others called it the "Over the Hill Club." I suppose some of us were getting on a bit!

The main member of this "Club" was the man of the house himself, Jack who sadly is no longer with us and we miss him very much. Jack did not say as much as some of the rest of us, but when he did speak, it was usually something worth saying. The most senior member now is Mick, no one knows exactly what age he is but he is now the "Fear-A-Tithe."

After Jack died we moved the gathering to Mick's house. Many people drop in, but the regulars are Paddy McGinley from Swillybrin, better known as Paddy Anton, Michael McGarvey (Mick's son) and myself. Teresa McGarvey (Mick's sister), who lives in Dublin, often visits for holidays and her contribution to the discussion gives us a women's outlook on many subjects. These nights can be very entertaining and even educational as many aspects of life in this country, and indeed the world, are discussed. Mick has a vast knowledge of local events and people who lived in the parish and other happenings (and indeed some things that never happened). All these qualities make him a very good storyteller. Mick has many sayings, but he has one that is very apt, with all the greed in society today and that is "too much of anything is na gid," (not good).

We often talked about starting our own website where people could log on and we could advise them on how to form such a group themselves. Our idea is that, instead of people going to a psychiatrist, they would form a group and talk about their problems and share each other's ideas. That was the reason people did not need any counselling in days gone by because they had very close contact with family and friends.

This talk may seem far-fetched and not very serious but it might not be very far off the mark. The raking nights that we have are reminiscence therapy at its best and are very beneficial for young and old. When I was growing up and in my teens, the word bored meant a hole bored in a piece of wood. We did not know of the word in any other context and thank God, as far as I am concerned it still means a hole made by woodworm or a drill.

Over the years many subjects and topics were discussed. The changes through the world over the last one hundred years were often talked about. Mick always held a belief that an invention as important as the wheel or the computer was still to be discovered. The build up for the new millennium began back about 1990 when all kinds of stories were being told about what was going to happen to the world when the second millennium would end. There were all the usual people putting out scary stories about the end of the world and all the tragedies that could befall people. Planes would fall out of the sky and ships and other things depending on computer control would all be in trouble. These discussions were a common occurrence on television programs and no one seemed to have the answer. Thankfully none of these things happened and everything is going along much the same as it did for the last two thousand years. Many nights were spent discussing the problems that would occur at the onset of the new millennium.

In saying that, great changes have taken place, even in my lifetime. I would consider that my generation saw more change than any other generation did in recent history. When I was a child, cars were very few and far between, as was any kind of mechanical vehicle. The biggest machine in the country areas was the old threshing mill. This machine was powered by two horses pulling a shaft around a special ring course. There were no mechanical diggers; all digging was done with a spade. In the 50's a one hundred ton dragline digger was being taken to Gweedore to clear an area of bog in preparation for the hydro electric scheme at Bunbeg. The machine got bogged down near Bunbeg and as they did not have a bigger machine to pull it out it was there for a few weeks. Any one who had a car would go over to Gweedore on a Sunday taking a few of their neighbours with them to see this machine. The radio was just beginning to become popular and the old gramophone was the main source of music. Air travel was unheard of in Ireland, except the planes that were used in the war. Counting was done in the head or on the fingers and the most sophisticated piece of counting equipment in the schools was the bar frame.

In my 70 odd years I have seen cars develop from very basic machines giving a lot of trouble, to the top of the range vehicles we have today. In that time I have witnessed men going to the moon and sending space ships far into space. Air travel is within the reach of everyone and people are now going on world cruises.

But, I think the biggest breakthrough of all has to be the technology of the computer.

In the year 1968 I attended an insurance course when I worked with New Ireland Assurance and they had installed their first computer. The machine covered a wall space of about 10 feet and had big reel tapes turning around everywhere on it. Today you could put a piece of equipment with a thousand times the memory of that computer in your pocket. The development of the silicon chip and its use in the world of computers has opened up all sorts of possibilities and has revolutionised the operation of machines and equipment everywhere.

Despite all this technology and modern ways of doing things there are some aspects of life that never change nor would we want them to. Families and family life I think are most important and thankfully in most country areas the family unit is of great importance.

We were fortunate that over the years our house was never without children. After our own children were grown up we would often look after neighbour's children. While the factory was going Tessie and myself would, at times, look after the children belonging to whoever would be the manager at the time. There was John and Maura Harvey and their three sons Paul, Mark and Peter. Then John and Carmel McCabe, had a son and daughter, Gillen and Hannah.

On a daily basis we also looked after Tessie's niece and nephew, Claire and Shaun Sweeney, while their mother Rosemary went to work. Then in later years, we had Sarah and David Valkenborghs, daughter and son of Hubert and Lucia Valkenborghs. Hubert is the son of Franz Valkenborghs who was the first manager of the veneer factory.

The nice thing about looking after children in this way is that they become very close and are like an extension to one's own family. That is particularly true with Sarah and David as they live just across the road and, even now they are grown up, they are still popping in and out all the time. Now we have our grandchildren, Orlaith, Tommy and Finn who visit us every day, and Jamie who comes over from London on holiday. I believe there is nothing as nice as having children around the house as it keeps you feeling younger and keeps you from thinking too much about yourself. As all grandparents know, you can have much more fun with your grandchildren than you had with your own children.

Chapter 20 - Ups and Downs.

Things happen throughout a lifetime, some joyful and some sad. Death is something that has to come to everyone and we all experience death in our families. Throughout my lifetime I have seen a number of deaths in the family, from my grandmother and grandfather to aunts and uncles, and my own father and mother. The death of a father and mother is always sad but when they have lived good lives and made it to a ripe old age as my father, who was 86 and my mother who was 84, you have much to be thankful for.

Two sad deaths I experienced was our son Pascal who died at birth in 1975, and my brother John who died in November 2005. Pascal never got a chance at life but we have the benefit of knowing that he is with God and is keeping an eye on the rest of us. John's death was unexpected and was the first break on the family. He lived in Co. Wicklow for many years but he loved his native Donegal and came here as often as he could.

After John died I missed him very much and it is still hard to accept that we will never enjoy his company again. John had a larger than life personality and was always interested in people, especially Donegal people. Growing up, I looked up to John and was very much influenced by him. He introduced me to the insurance business and encouraged me to always think positively and to have confidence in my own ability. As a result of that I always tried to think positively in all aspects of life.

Another sad death was my younger brother Hugh's wife, Mary, who died in 2003. Mary was from Kilkenny, her and Hugh and their family lived in Dublin. Mary was a young woman and she loved to come to Donegal on holidays and we all miss her very much, especially when it comes to family events and any of the holiday times like summer and Christmas.

But as life has its down periods so it also has up periods and it is important that the two balance. As I am coming to the more mature years of my life, I have good reason to count my blessings. Tessie and myself are happy in the knowledge that we have a good family and are thankful that we have had good health, apart from a few little blips, to enjoy our family growing up.

The 1980's was a bad time in Ireland for employment, especially Donegal, and we were plunged back to the old days of emigration. In 1987 two of our family, Leo and Mark, left school and could find no work here, so it was off to London for them. One year later it was the same for our only daughter, Edel. Paul was a few years younger than them and he continued his education by going to university in Galway where he graduated with a degree in Community Development and went to work in Manchester. He went to Australia where he spent three years but is now back working in Dublin. James is the one member of the family who never really emigrated although he did work in Dublin and Belfast as well as doing a short period in Leeds.

Three of our family Leo, Mark and James are now married and we are blessed with four grandchildren – three grandsons and one granddaughter. Our oldest son Leo, married Janet Beston from near Bowness on Windermere in the Lake District of Cumbria. Mark married Donna Perry from a place called Crewkerne in Somerset. James did not go too far to get a wife, you could say she is the girl next door. She is from the next townland, Ballymore, her name is Donna Montgomery.

James and Donna have built a house at home and it's nice to have them living beside us. Leo and Janet have also built a house beside us so we have the privilege of having three of our grandchildren here all the time, Leo and Janet's son Finn, and James and Donna's daughter Orlaith and new son Tommy. Mark's son Jamie lives in London but he comes over here two or three times every year. Mark is still into the music and is doing gigs around London. When they all went to London in 1987 they thought they were all going to be rock stars but I think Mark is now content to be playing with his band around the pubs in London and who knows where it might lead. Edel is still in London and has a great job but hopes to come home shortly and build a house.

We had a lovely visit to Australia in March 2006; it was the holiday of a lifetime. We spent a month with Paul and travelled around New South Wales and visited all the beauty spots in that part of Australia. At that time Paul worked with Barnardo's, which includes working with the Aboriginal people around Sydney.

I am conscious of the fact that I never had to emigrate and I thank God for that. While I travelled to many countries on holidays and playing music, I never had to work away from home to earn a living. I composed a song around that fact.

AT HOME ON MY DONEGAL SHORE
I've never sailed over the ocean,
Nor left my own native home,
I've never been sad or downhearted
In a far foreign land o'er the foam.
I have stayed on the spot I was born in,

And married the girl next door
And I'm happy to say I enjoyed every day,
Here at home on my Donegal shore.
I grew up in a land full of beauty,
'Round Creeslough and Marble Hill,
Where we'd swim in the long summer evening,
My thoughts go back to it still.
Then we'd meet with the girls and go dancing,
To Milford or maybe the west,
But wherever we'd roam we'd always come home,
For the Creeslough hall was the best.
The long winter nights I remember,
Through the houses we'd ramble along,
'Round the big turf fire we'd gather,
And listen to story and song.
Then the old folk would tell of the old times,
And things that happened thon time,
But now sure we are the old folk,
And we give the young the same line.
And now as I sit here and ponder,
In the autumn years of my life,
I think of the happy and full life we had
With the girl I took for my wife.
And the old house is still standing,
And the roses are all growing tall,
So if you're passing by, don't ever be shy,
There's a welcome there when you call.

It is heartening for Tessie and myself, after almost twenty years of having only one member of the family at home, to see the rest of them starting to return. Leo and James are now helping me with the undertaking business and will eventually carry on the business themselves.

In September of 2006 I had another little problem with the old heart and had an ICD installed. This device works like a pacemaker but also has a built in defibrillator. Please God this piece of equipment will keep me going for another few years, and who knows, I might even get another book on paper.

In February 2007 I saw the big machines knocking down the old veneer factory, which opened in 1960. It was knocked down to make way for the building of five houses. In a way it was sad to see it being taken away as it holds many memories for many people. The factory created employment for a lot of people from the Creeslough and Dunfanaghy area for over 20 years. My mother ran a little shop while the factory was open which was a good source of income for her and my father.

But things have to move on and I suppose you could say it was one of those things that did its job at a time when the country was being built up. Nothing lasts forever. However, I think there are too many houses being built in the country areas, especially holiday homes. They tend to be empty most of the time and the only thing you can see on a winter's night is a row of doorbell lights.

Chapter 21 – Fiddles and other hobbies

Throughout this book you have read my account of different jobs I embarked upon during my life. When I left national school, which was the only school I attended, I went to a woodwork class. This gave me an interest in carpentry and all sorts of woodwork. This meant I did all my own woodwork and some for others too. Electrics was another trade I did in a small way in the early years, before you had to be a qualified person to wire houses. Plumbing and central heating I studied through books and was able to do my own work when I built the first part of our house in the early 1960's. In my spare time I did some plumbing work for some of the neighbours. During the end of the 1970's and into the 1980's I started restoring old furniture and learned about French polishing and other restoration techniques, which I developed and became quite good at.

Through my association with the veneer factory I became well informed on all sorts of exotic woods. The factory imported all kinds of hardwood timber from Africa so I gained valuable information in handling and working with most of these timbers.

All my life I've been around violins, or fiddles as we call them. From about 1980 I started buying and selling old violins. Again, through books and experience, I gained quite a bit of knowledge about these old fiddles and did repairs for students and other people who needed their old fiddles restored. I have met a lot of people over the years through my fiddles.

Antique furniture was very rewarding work. There was nothing as nice as to see a piece of fine furniture coming back to it's full glory after being lying up for years, covered in dirt and grime. To see the glow of red mahogany or golden oak coming through is wonderful. Then to stand back and admire the beauty of it and marvel at the skill with which it was made, maybe 150 years ago.

But nothing compares to with putting the final touches to an old violin. I have often bought old violins that must have been played in country houses for upwards of one hundred years. These violins were played at all kinds of parties and at the American wakes, which was the party held for people going to America in the 1920's and 1930's. They were played at weddings and dances. They may have played sad laments at wakes and funerals. This instrument which had evoked such a range of emotion was now covered in soot and falling apart.

After a few weeks of gluing and cleaning the instrument is ready for stringing up. Pegs, bridge, fingerboard and a tailpiece are fitted before putting in place the heart and soul of the violin. This little stick of fine-grained pine is stood inside the fiddle under the second string and just a little bit behind the bridge and is called the sound post.

Throughout the restoration of the fiddle so much loving care, skill and attention has gone into the work and the big moment is imminent. I put on a set of new strings and tune them up. This is the moment of truth, I will hear for the first time, what kind of sound will be produced. This may be the first sound this fiddle has made in fifty years.

The first sound will not be the best as a violin that has not been played for a long time will take a lot of playing to bring it to its best sound. Just to be able to play a tune on it and see its old timber shining through the texture of its golden varnish is ample reward. I know that, over time, the fiddle will come back to its former glory. Talking about old fiddles and former glory, it is a myth that an old fiddle is always good. If an old fiddle was a bad fiddle two hundred years ago it is an even worse fiddle today.

The antique furniture and violin restoration were mainly just hobbies. Another hobby I always had ainterest in was photography. When I travelled around the country selling insurance I always carried a camera and captured many good scenes in the countryside. In those years it was an expensive hobby as film and development were expensive. I would have loved to develop my own photographs but it meant getting a lot of equipment and, as I said, everything to do with it cost a lot of money. However, when digital cameras and digital processing on computers came along, I was able to fulfil my ambition. I already had a computer so I picked up a digital camera and, armed with that, and Photoshop, I was in business. It was no time until I could put people in and take people out, open eyes and put people or anything else in places where they never were. Of course anyone with a computer and the right software knows how easy it is to do all that.

This reminds me of a story my father used to tell. In his day it was thought to be a very far-fetched story. The story was of a woman who was visiting her son in London and she went to a photographer to get a picture done up a bit. She explained to the man that this was the only picture she had of her late husband so she would like to get it brightened up and make some changes. He asked her what changes she wanted and she said she would like if he could take that old dirty cap off his head. He said he could do that and that it would be ready in three days. She thanked him and was leaving when the man asked her what side her husband parted his hair on and the woman replied, "Sure you will see that when you take the cap off." Little did my father know just how easy that job would be, not that many years later.

Chapter 22 – In the Community

Throughout my lifetime I have been involved in, I suppose one could say, the life of the parish. My first introduction to parish activities was at about the age of ten, serving Mass for Fr Tom Gallagher in the old chapel of Doe, which is now demolished.

In those days the old chapel did not have electricity so there was no heating. The light was provided by tilley lamps. Everything was very basic with the stone flag floor, big pine seats and bare hard kneelers. It was the custom then for the men to stay on one side and the women on the other, which made it very embarrassing for a young lad who thought he was too big to have to go into a seat with his mother. When a couple got married, it was the custom for the couple to go into the one seat together on their first Sunday as man and wife. He was a "brave" man who would continue to accompany his wife into the same seat every Sunday after that. It was not until the 1960's that this custom was done away with and men and women mixed through the chapel.

I have good memories of Fr Tom. He was a very friendly priest and was always telling us stories about when he was in Australia. He once took me to see the oldest woman in the parish. She lived in Derryreel on the west side of the parish, not far from the neighbouring parish of Cloughanealy. Her name was Doohan. This old lady was 105 years and Fr Tom said to me "I want you to see her as you may never see anyone as old again," and he was right, I have never seen as old a person since. She lived for two more years when she died at the age of 107 years. She was the oldest person in the parish for at least one hundred years. The nearest to that was Jim Shields from Kilmacloo, Creeslough, who died at 104.

I served Mass for Fr Tom up until 1949 when we got a new priest whose name was Fr James Deeney, originally from Rathmullen. Fr Deeney was a completely different type of person from Fr Tom, a much younger man and very strict. I was selling papers after Mass on Sundays and to do that I had to leave before Mass ended. As that was not acceptable to Fr Deeney, I had to make a choice. I was fourteen years of age then and getting a bit old to be serving Mass, so I retired as a server.

Fr James Deeney was a very progressive priest and was very much ahead of his time. The first thing he did was to move all the men who had a habit of standing at the back of the chapel, and some of them out in the porch on their one knee, right up the floor and into a seat. The Mass then was said in Latin so nobody knew what the priest was saying, but Fr Deeney taught the congregation to answer the Mass in Latin and, as soon as it was allowed to say the Mass in English, he had lay people doing the readings. I would say we were the first parish in the Dioceses to have lay readers.

Before the new church was built in Creeslough, Mass was celebrated in Glassan and Drimnaraw schools on alternate weeks. He would say mass facing the people, and this was before the Second Vatican Council. I always had great respect for Fr Deeney as he had some very good, sound ideas and he always looked for high standards and was very devout. I think if Fr Deeney had any fault it was that he set his standards too high which made some people feel they were impossible to achieve.

Fr Deeney was not too long in the parish when he started the Pioneer Total Abstinence Association. The object of being a full member of the "Pioneers" was to promise to abstain from all alcoholic drink for life. That might seem to be a very big commitment but it was not long until most young people took "the pledge" as it was known.

During the 1950's and 1960's it was the popular thing to have taken the pledge. The word "cool" did not exist then, except to describe weather, but if it had, then being a pioneer would be cool. It just goes to show that if the right standards are set young people will respond. I became a pioneer in 1951 and I am still a member today and I can say I never felt the need to take alcoholic drink. That said, I have nothing against people who enjoy a drink, as I spent many years playing music in pubs.

Fr Deeney also introduced the Legion of Mary to the parish, and my brother John was one of the founding members. Everyone thought it was a woman's organisation but he started it off with men and then when he had eight men enrolled, he took in the ladies. I joined the Legion of Mary in 1957 and remained a member until about 1970. The Legion was a very good organisation and did a lot of very good work throughout the parish. It was also an excellent opportunity for young people to be trained in many aspects of parish activities and helped them get an in-depth knowledge of their faith.

While my own family was growing up I retired from the Legion of Mary as I thought family commitments were more important. But, I never strayed too far from parish activities and was always involved in different committees.

In 1971 a new church was built in Creeslough. The new church took the same name as the old Doe Chapel in Cashelmore, St Michael The Archangel. It was built in Creeslough as it was more central and it was thought that, as it was close to the village of Creeslough, it would have more people calling to say a prayer during the weekdays. Fr Deeney died in 1983 and is buried in Rathmullen. The next priest we had was Fr Colton who was followed by Fr Connaghan, and then Fr Crossan. After him was Fr Friel and at the present time we have Fr Briody.

In 1984 I became a member of The Society of St Vincent de Paul, popularly known as SVP. Fredric Ozanam founded the SVP in France in the year 1833 and it has since spread throughout the world. The SVP does a lot of very good work and while the nature of the work has changed over the years, it is still focused on helping the less-well-off in society. People might think, in the midst of all the wealth we have in the country today, that there is not as much need for the likes of the SVP but they would be wrong. The fact is that there are more people now finding it difficult to support their family due to high prices, especially housing. The fact that the SVP is such a large organisation and has a very strong voice enables them to play a very important role in lobbying the government for better social welfare structures and other legislation.

In 1991 the SVP in Creeslough was asked by then councillor, Noel McGinley, if we would take on a project to build houses for the elderly as well as a day centre. After some discussion, we agreed to take on the project. A grant of 90% was available for such a project and only a voluntary organisation such as the SVP could avail of the grant. This was something new then and it was a big challenge to us.

At the setting up of this scheme we worked very closely with the North Western Health Board. Our main contact person was Mr Ken Sharpe who had an office in St Connals hospital, where Ken and myself had many a pleasant meeting. I must say we could not have had a more co-operative and helpful man than Ken. We decided to build a community day centre and 14 houses for the elderly. The site belonged to the health board and they transferred it over to us for the project. The houses and day centre were officially opened in 1997.

The houses are now fully occupied and the day centre is opened three days every week. The whole scheme has been of great value to the area. Around thirty senior citizens go to the day centre every day where they are fed and entertained. They make new friends and chat to each other, which is very important in alleviating loneliness.

Another aspect of this kind of scheme is that when elderly people are living in an environment like this, where there is a caretaker going around day and night looking after their needs, they feel safe and happy. It has been my experience that when people, especially older people, are content and happy, they are also much healthier. The end result of that is people living like this are less likely have to go to a nursing home. This project was a bright spot in my life and I got immense satisfaction and fulfilment from being part of a combined effort to enhance the community and add to the life of the parish.

Chapter 23 - Thank you and Goodnight

Like any story the ending is the hardest part to get right. Did you ever listen to a clergyman preach a sermon on Sunday and he is doing very well until he has the main story told, he then begins to labour the point as he struggles with the ending? You are sitting there, thinking "Why does he not finish when he is ahead?" Well, I hope I will take my own advice when it comes to the ending of this story.

Looking back at my life, I have many things to be thankful for. As a couple, Tessie and I came through all the ups and downs of life but, thank God, we remember the good times the best.

After bringing up a family and going through all the different aspects of a family growing up, getting married and some moving far from home, it is nice to relax and reflect on the past. It is also nice to know that as the couple who started the whole thing off we are still together for each other and the family. Now we like to think we are retired, well semi-retired anyway, and we have time to sit back and let other people do the work. One of the nice things of being at our stage of life is that we are freer to do things together now, than earlier in life; because of other commitments.

Throughout this story I talked about people in the old days helping their family and their neighbour and in this year of 2008 I am pleased to say it still happens, in Donegal anyhow. I am glad to be able to end on a happy note and to say how pleased we are that our family are starting to return home after many years away. That has to be an improvement on the stories told in the old emigration songs where the son went away and never returned. So, please God, we can now look forward to the rest of our lives with our children and grandchildren around us.

Well, that's my story as it happened …. and it took a lifetime.

Other books and Recordings by this Author

Single "Maid of Marble Hill" 1980

"Poets AND People of Doe" 1996

"As I See It" 1968

Co-author "The Disappearing Irish Cottage" 2004

Record single "Maid of Marble Hill" 1980

Album "Quality of Life" 1992

Album "At home on my Donegal Shore" 1999